T0213041

Whitestein Series in Software Agent Technologies and Autonomic Computing

Series Editors:
Marius Walliser
Stefan Brantschen
Monique Calisti
Stefan Schinkinger

This series reports new developments in agent-based software technologies and agent-oriented software engineering methodologies, with particular emphasis on applications in the area of autonomic computing & communications.

The spectrum of the series includes research monographs, high quality notes resulting from research and industrial projects, outstanding Ph.D. theses, and the proceedings of carefully selected conferences. The series is targeted at promoting advanced research and facilitating know-how transfer to industrial use.

About Whitestein Technologies

Whitestein Technologies is a leading innovator in the area of software agent technologies and autonomic computing & communications. Whitestein Technologies' offering includes advanced products, solutions, and services for various applications and industries, as well as a comprehensive middleware for the development and operation of autonomous, self-managing, and self-organizing systems and networks.
Whitestein Technologies' customers and partners include innovative global enterprises, service providers, and system integrators, as well as universities, technology labs, and other research institutions.

www.whitestein.com

Agent Technology and e-Health

Roberta Annicchiarico
Ulises Cortés
Cristina Urdiales
Editors

Birkhäuser
Basel · Boston · Berlin

Editors:

Roberta Annicchiarico
Fondazione Santa Lucia IRCCS
Via Ardeatina 306
00179 Roma
Italy
r.annicchiarico@hsantalucia.it

Ulises Cortés
Departamento Software
Universidad Polytècnica de Catalunya
C. Jordi Girona 1-3
08034 Barcelona
Spain
ia@lsi.upc.edu

Cristina Urdiales
Departamento Tecnologia ETSI Telecomunicacion
Universidad Malaga
Campus de Teatinos
29071 Malaga
Spain
cris@dte.uma.es

2000 Mathematical Subject Classification: 68T05, 68T30

Library of Congress Control Number: 2007938078

Bibliographic information published by Die Deutsche Bibliothek
Die Deutsche Bibliothek lists this publication in the Deutsche Nationalbibliografie;
detailed bibliographic data is available in the Internet at <http://dnb.ddb.de>.

ISBN 978-3-7643-8546-0 Birkhäuser Verlag AG, Basel – Boston – Berlin

© 2008 Birkhäuser Verlag, P.O. Box 133, CH-4010 Basel, Switzerland
Part of Springer Science+Business Media
Printed on acid-free paper produced from chlorine-free pulp. TCF ∞
Printed in Germany

ISBN 978-3-7643-8546-0   e-ISBN 978-3-7643-8547-7

9 8 7 6 5 4 3 2 1   www.birkhauser.ch

Contents

Whitestein Series in Software Agent Technologies, 1–4
© 2007 Birkhäuser Verlag Basel/Switzerland

Agents and Healthcare: Usability and Acceptance

Ulises Cortés, Roberta Annicchiarico and Cristina Urdiales

1. Introduction

Agent technology has become a leading area of research in AI and computer science and the focus of a number of major initiatives [5]. The interest in applying Artificial Intelligence technologies first, and now Agent Technology to Healthcare has been a growing one. From the very seminal and inspiring work as the one of Huang *et al.* [1] and [2] the use of agents in Healthcare has been continuously evolving and covering more aspects. Intelligent Agents are normally used to observe the current situation and knowledge base, and then support the expert's decision-making on an action consistent with the domain they are in, and finally perform the execution of that action on the environment. This evolution brought the creation of steady series of workshops where a growing community has been joining to put together the latest advancements in the field see, for example [7, 8, 5, 6] and also major AI journals devote special issues to this field as for example [4, 3].

This evolution shows that this community is able to deploy Multi-Agent Systems (MAS) that nowadays are acting in a diversity of applications to Healthcare. For example, there are multiple areas in the Medical Industry that would benefit from Agent-based systems designed to support a range of decisions from Diagnosis Assistants, to Treatment recommending systems, to Patient History Examination Systems, the support of Palliative Care Units, *etc.*

The healthcare environment in the actual world consists of vast amounts of dynamic and unstructured information, distributed over a large number of formal (and informal) information systems [10]. Agent Technology is having an ever-growing impact on the delivery of medical information. It supports acquiring and manipulating information distributed in a large number of information systems.

Authors would like to acknowledge support from the *SHARE-it*: Supported Human Autonomy for Recovery and Enhancement of cognitive and motor abilities using information technologies (FP6-IST-045088). The views expressed in this paper are not necessarily those of *SHARE-it* consortium.

Moreover is suitable for the computer untrained medical stuff. The features of intelligent agents are aimed at distributing the task of solving problems, by allowing different software components to cooperate, each one with its own expertise. Patient management has been thus far the best experimented application of intelligent agents in Healthcare because of the inherently distributed nature of the expertise needed for that problem but nowadays the range of applications covers the whole spectrum. Healthcare information systems can use agent-oriented cooperation techniques and standardized, electronic healthcare-record-exchange protocols to combine information about the different facets of a patient's therapy provided by different healthcare providers at different locations.

Healthcare systems seem to be an environment suitable for the Multiagent Systems (MAS): they are composed by complex systems with heterogeneous components, managing distributed data and resources, and often needs integration with heterogeneous legacy systems (such as hospital/laboratory information systems). In addition, healthcare professionals experience a high level of mobility because they must collaborate with colleagues and access information and artifacts distributed throughout the premises. Telemedicine systems are a special case to be considered as they are crucially based on continuously appearing and disappearing components, with distributed features.

Because ever more powerful intelligent agents, from now on agents, will interact with people in increasingly sophisticated and important ways, greater attention must be given to the technical and social aspects of *how* to make agents acceptable, sound and safe to people. This is specially true when agents are created to deal with humans' health care and/or to support humans to perform their Activities of Daily Life in an autonomous way. Those issues are rarely addressed by the Agents' research community.

2. The papers in this collection

The set of papers in this collection was selected among the contributions to the 4th *Workshop on Agents Applied in Health Care* (AAH'2006) held at the European Conference on Artificial Intelligence (ECAI2006) [6]. Multi-Agent Systems are one of the most exciting research areas in Artificial Intelligence. In the last ten years there has been a growing interest in the application of agent-based systems in health care. Moreover, a growing European community of researchers interested in the application of intelligent agents in Healthcare emerged as a result of the activities within the AgentCities.NET European network and the AgentLink III Technical Forum Group on Healthcare Applications of Intelligent Agents. And specially in R&D projects funded under the Framework Program VI (FP6).

All the contributions to this collection describe the research carried out in some of the R&D projects funded by the European Union under the FP6, some of them are still active. This selection gives the reader a flavor of the most actual research in Europe in the field of Agents applied to Healthcare. This book reports on the results achieved in this area, discusses the benefits (and drawbacks) that Agent-Based systems may bring to medical domains and society, and also to provide a list of the research topics that should be tackled in the near future to make the deployment of Healthcare agent-based systems a reality.

Current topics of research include communication and co-operation between distributed intelligent agents to manage patient care, information agents that retrieve medical information from the Internet, and multi-agent systems that assist the doctors in the tasks of monitoring and diagnosis.

The papers in this volume are:

- *HealthAgents: Agent-based Distributed Decision Support System for Brain Tumour Diagnosis and Prognosis.*
- *SAPHIRE: A Multi-Agent System for Remote Healthcare Monitoring through Computerized Clinical Guidelines.*
- *Applying Provenance in Distributed Organ Transplant Management.*
- *ASPIC: Argumentation Service Platform with Integrated Components.*
- *K4CARE: Knowledge-Based HomeCare eServices for an Ageing Europe.*
- *Supported Human Autonomy for Recovery and Enhancement of cognitive and motor disabilities using Agent technologies.*

References

[1] I. Huang and N. R. Jennings and J. Fox. *An agent-based approach to healthcare management.* Int. J. Appl. Artif. Intell., vol. 9, pp. 401420,1995.

[2] J.E. Larssan and B. Hayes-Roth *Guardian: intelligent autonomous agent for medical monitoring and diagnosis.* IEEE Intelligent Systems. 13(1): p. 58-64. 1998

[3] A. Moreno (Editor). *On the evolution of applying Agent Technology to Healthcare.* IEEE Intelligent Systems. 21(6). 2006.

[4] A. Moreno and C. Garbay C. (Editors) *Software agents in health care.* Artificial Intelligence in Medecine. 27(3):229-32. 2003.

[5] A. Moreno and J. Nealon (Editors) *Applications of Software Agents Technology in the Health Care Domain.* Whitestein series in software agent technology. Birkhuser Verlag AG. 2003. ISBN: 978-3-7643-2662-3

[6] A. Moreno. and R. Annicchiarico and. U. Cortés. *4th Workshop on Agents Applied in Health Care* (AAH'2006). European Conference on Artificial Intelligence. Riva del Garda. Italy.

[7] J. Nealon and A. Moreno, *The application of agent technology to health care*, Proceedings of the Workshop AgentCities: Research in Large-scale Open Agent Environments, in the 1st International Joint Conference on Autonomous Agents and Multi-Agent Systems (AAMAS 02), p. 169-73, Bologna, Italy, 2002.

[8] J. Nealon (Editor) *Agents applied to Healthcare.* AI Communications 18(2005):171-173.

[9] M. E. Polack. *Intelligent Technology for an Aging Population: The Use of AI to Assist Elders with Cognitive Impairment.* AI Magazine. 26(2):9-24. 2005.

[10] R.M. Vicari and C.D. Flores and A.M. Silvestre L.J. Seixas and M. Ladeira and H. Coelho *A multi-agent intelligent environment for medical knowledge.* Artificial Intelligence in Medicine. 27(3): p. 335-366. 2003.

Ulises Cortés
Technical University of Catalonia
Omega 135. Jordi Girona 1 & 3
Barcelona 08034
Spain
e-mail: ia@lsi.upc.edu

Roberta Annicchiarico
Fondazione Santa Lucia
Via Ardetina 306
00179 Roma
Italia
e-mail: r.annicchiarico@hsantalucia.it

Cristina Urdiales
University of Malaga
Departamento Tecnología Electrónica, E.T.S.I. Telecomunicación, Campus de Teatinos
29071 Málaga
Spain
e-mail: acurdiales@uma.es

Whitestein Series in Software Agent Technologies, 5–24
© 2007 Birkhäuser Verlag Basel/Switzerland

On the Implementation of HEALTHAGENTS: Agent-Based Brain Tumour Diagnosis

Magí Lluch-Ariet, Francesc Estanyol, Mariola Mier, Carla Delgado, Horacio González–Vélez, Tiphaine Dalmas, Montserrat Robles, Carlos Sáez, Javier Vicente, Sabine Van Huffel, Jan Luts, Carles Arús, Ana Paula Candiota Silveira, Margarida Julià–Sapé, Andrew Peet, Alex Gibb, Yu Sun, Bernardo Celda, Maria Carmen Martínez Bisbal, Giulia Valsecchi, David Dupplaw, Bo Hu and Paul Lewis

Abstract. This paper introduces HealthAgents, an EC-funded research project to improve the classification of brain tumours through multi-agent decision support over a secure and distributed network of local databases or Data Marts. HealthAgents will not only develop new pattern recognition methods for distributed classification and analysis of in vivo MRS and ex vivo/in vitro HRMAS and DNA data, but also define a method to assess the quality and usability of a new candidate local database containing a set of new cases, based on a compatibility score. Using its Multi-Agent architecture, HealthAgents intends to apply cutting-edge agent technology to the Biomedical field and develop the HealthAgents network, a globally distributed information and knowledge repository for brain tumour diagnosis and prognosis.

Keywords. Distributed Healthcare Systems; Brain Tumours; Oncology; Decision-Support Systems; Agent Technology ; Medical Informatics; Computer-Based Medical Systems.

1. Introduction

Brain tumours remain a prevalent cause of morbidity and mortality in Europe [5]. Even though it is not the most common type of cancer, brain tumours account for a greater proportion of tumours in younger age groups than other types of tumour. They are thus a significant cause of cancer in young adults and children. Indeed, brain tumours are the most common solid malignancies in children.

Special thanks from the HealthAgents Consortium to Carla Delgado and Ewen Maclean who put together the contributions from several colleagues in the consortium in order to build this text.

FIGURE 1. HealthAgents Conceptual model.

Nowadays the diagnosis and treatment of brain tumours is typically based on clinical symptoms, radiological appearance and often a histopathological diagnosis of a biopsy. However, treatment response of histologically or radiologically-similar tumours can vary widely, particularly in children. Magnetic Resonance Spectroscopy (MRS) is a non-invasive technique for determining the tissue biochemical composition (metabolomic profile) of a tumour. Additionally, the genomic profile, determined using DNA microarrays, facilitates the classification of tumour grades and types not trivially distinguished by morphologic appearance. Diagnosis using Magnetic Resonance Imaging (MRI) is non-invasive, but only achieves 60-90% accuracy depending on the tumour type and grade. The current gold standard classification of brain tumours by biopsy and histopathological analysis involves invasive surgical procedure and incurs a significant risk.

Thus, the HealthAgents project [30], [1] entails the development of a web-based decision support system (DSS) which employs MRS and genomic profiles. This DSS will deploy an agent-based architecture in order to provide a distributed diagnostic tool for brain tumours, implement data mining techniques, transfer clinical data and extract information. The distributed nature of our approach will help the users to observe local centre policies for sharing information whilst allowing them to benefit from the use of a distributed data warehouse (d-DWH). Moreover, it will permit the design of local classifiers targeting a specific patient population.

This new information for classifying tumours along with clinical data should be securely and easily accessible in order to improve the diagnosis and prognosis of tumours. All data will be stored anonymously and securely, through a network of data marts based on the acquired information and stored at centres throughout Europe. This network will grant bona-fide access to an organisation in return for its contribution of clinical data to a d-DWH/Decision Support System (d-DSS).

The HealthAgents system presents an approach that builds upon previous experiences in biomedical informatics, particularly in image processing and computer-aided diagnosis [12]; in machine learning for brain tumour classification using MRS [11]; and in agents' architecture [22] .

By the time this text is being written, HealthAgents is in the second of its three years of development. Though the system is not yet finished, relevant achievements have already been accomplished, including the construction of the first prototype of the DSS, which is comprised of an agent-based architecture, with an associated ontology, data mining techniques, and protocols for clinical data exchange [10].

The following sections describe the HealthAgents project and its current state – first, we provide some background on the underlying technologies for this project: brain tumour diagnosis and agent technology. Also, we present some related work. Section 3 describes the HealthAgents architectural specification, section 4 describes the HealthAgents classifiers system, section 5 describes the Data Entry and section 6 provides the status of the already implemented prototype of the HealthAgents system. In section 7 we report some evaluation results; future work and conclusions are stated in sections 8 and 9 respectively.

2. Background

2.1. Brain Tumour Diagnosis

Brain tumours remain an important cause of morbidity and mortality and afflict an increasing percentage of aging adults with a crude incidence rate of 8 per 100,000 inhabitants in Europe [5]. In children over 1 year of age, brain tumours are the most common solid malignancies that cause disease-related death.

Diagnosis using Magnetic Resonance Imaging (MRI) is non-invasive, but only a-chieves 60-90% accuracy depending on the tumour type and grade [14]. The current gold standard classification of a brain tumour by histopathological analysis of a biopsy, is an invasive surgical procedure and incurs a risk of 2.4-3.5% morbidity and 0.2-0.8% mortality, in addition to healthcare costs and stress to patients. For tumours that evolve slowly (e.g. pilocytic astrocytoma in children), repeated biopsies may not be advisable or practical. There is a need to improve brain tumour classification, and to provide non-invasive methods for brain tumour diagnosis and prognosis, to aid patient management and treatment. Three techniques are available to address these needs:

1. Magnetic Resonance Spectroscopy (MRS) [13] is a non-invasive technique that provides biochemical information on tissue in vivo.
2. HR-MAS [20, 2] is applied to biopsies in vitro in order to improve characterisation. Also, DNA microarray analysis of biopsies can determine tumour phenotype from gene expression profiles and predict better survival than classical histology [24, 23].
3. MRS, coupled with conventional MRI, provides metabolite profiles of a single voxel (SV) of tumour tissue [28, 13] (see Fig. 2). It also produces a molecular image of particular tumour metabolites in 10 minutes using multi-voxel (MV) techniques (Fig. 3).

2.2. Agent technology

Several modern complex distributed systems are composed of customisable building blocks, known as agents. Surveys on agent technology enumerate four important characteristics of agent technology [7]. First, agents possess an internal knowledge-based state that can be dynamically altered. Second, they have dynamic reasoning capabilities that determine their internal behaviour through constraints or goals. Third, they sustain a communication status that enables them to interact with agents or human entities. Last, they feature a unique identity that provides roaming and service advertising capabilities.

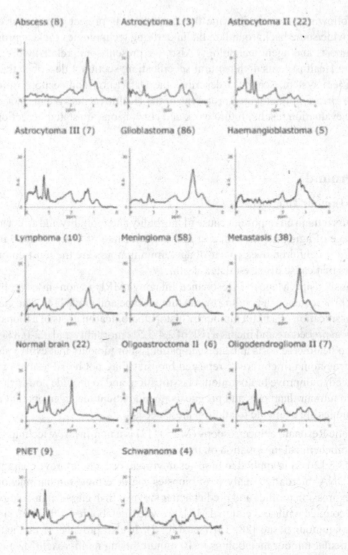

FIGURE 2. Mean short echo spectra of representative pathologies in a validated-DB from the INTERPRET project [15]. These were obtained by averaging spectra normalised to the Euclidian norm. The vertical axis is displayed in the same arbitrary units (a.u.) scale for all types. The horizontal axis labels ppm values with the number of cases of each type in parentheses. The most relevant metabolites are: lipids, 0.9 and 1.29 ppm; N-acetyl-containing compounds, 2.03 ppm; acetate, 1.9 ppm; macromolecules and glutamate/glutamine containing compounds, 2-2.5 ppm; creatine, 3.03 ppm; choline-containing compounds, 3.21 ppm; myo-inositol and glycine, 3.55 ppm; glutamate/glutamine-containing compounds and alanine, 3.77 ppm. (Adapted from Figure 4 of [28] ©2006 John Wiley & Sons Limited. Reproduced with permission.)

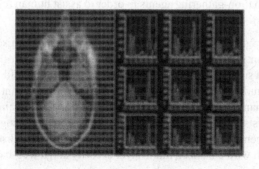

(a)

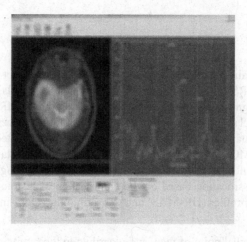

(b)

FIGURE 3. (a) Molecular image of Cho (choline) concentration distribution from CSI spectra of a patient with a Glioblastoma (red indicates highest Cho levels in the tumour) including the deconvoluted spectrum. (b) CSI spectra from the rear cavity with a demyelisation lesion. The nine spectra shown, from the selected green square, present the most abnormal region bottom right (Images generated using SIView 2.0 [19])

Extensive research in agent systems has been conducted in Europe, as demonstrated by the reach of the AgentLink membership [33]. Data mining agents present human researchers with a set of potential hypotheses deduced from the data sources. Thus, with the information explosion caused by genomics and proteomics research, there is a great need for automated information-gathering agents in order to assist human researchers conducting automated or semi-automated testing of data.

Recent initiatives have introduced the use of agents and web services to genome analysis and decision support in the biomedical sciences [21]. On the other hand, the design of web-based support has evolved into a mature research field for the integration of domain specific studies with computer science [35]. However, scant multi-disciplinary research has been channelled to the distributed bioinformatics domain, where numerous databases and analysis tools are independently administered in geographically distinct localities, lending themselves almost ideally to the adoption of a distributed intelligent multi-agent approach with enhanced multi-layer security and a web-based user interface.

2.3. Related work

A centralised DSS is already available from the INTERPRET project [32, 15] to facilitate the clinical use of MRS in brain tumour diagnosis which uses a classification based on histopathological diagnosis. A more elaborated DSS, combining MRS biochemical profiles from Single Voxel (SV) and metabolic spatial distribution by Chemical Shift Imaging (CSI) MRS in vivo data, is currently being developed and implemented in the eTUMOUR project [9]. The eTUMOUR DSS will eventually improve and facilitate the clinical application of MRS in adults and paediatric brain tumour diagnosis, prognosis and treatment selection using a classification based on the combination of histology results and high resolution metabolic profiles (HR-MAS) and transcriptomic (DNA micro-arrays) ex vivo data.

From the biological point of view and regarding to the brain tumour diagnosis domain, as it was pointed in [32], it soon became apparent in INTERPRET that there would not be enough cases available for performing a PR analysis of each of the approximately 100 tumour types and tumour-like lesions of the WHO classification of brain tumours [18]. One illustrative example can be that of craniopharingiomas, with an incidence of 1.3 cases per 1,000,000 persons per year [8]. From a practical point of view, if a classifier for this tumour type is to be developed, there are only two solutions: wait a large number of years in order to gather sufficient number of data or gather all data from as many craniopharyngioma cases around the world, test for compatibility among them and develop a classifier from these distributed data. This second solution would be the ideal environment in which an agent-based solution could be applied.

The HealthAgents d-DSS will build upon these projects and include additional MRS data, such as childhood tumours and less common adult tumours, using new classifications based on genetics. The development of this new d-DWH (the "d-DSS"), incorporating concepts of networking, agent technology, and data mining, must increase the number of accessible cases, yielding to a set of improved classifiers.

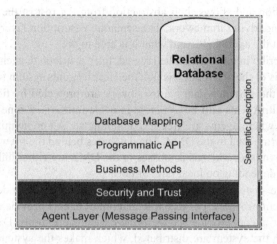

FIGURE 4. HealthAgents (multi-layer framework)

3. Architectural specification

By focusing on brain tumour diagnosis and prognosis, the HealthAgents project is intended to apply agent technology to securely connect user sites with a distributed database. It will employ agent negotiation and argumentation mechanisms developed for distributed resource allocation problems.

Moreover, HealthAgents intends to build a completely distributed repository with local databases. Grid technologies such as multi-site data partition and distributed data sharing will permit the seamless access to different databases across sites.

We argue that a d-DSS will furnish a completely new approach to brain tumour diagnosis. Since inferences from local predictions may well conflict with one another, reasoned argument between intelligent agents, acting on behalf of scientists, in a multi-agent system, will foster consensus.

The HealthAgents project intends to apply agent technology to the biomedical field in a multi-disciplinary fashion, and also develop the first distributed repository for brain tumour diagnosis, leading eventually to the formation of a special interest data grid.

HealthAgents proposes a multi-layer system architecture as depicted in Fig. 3. The database-mapping layer is used to map a relational database schema to the HealthAgents ontological schema. The programming API layer abstracts the underlying database interaction from the agent architecture. The business methods layer contributes to the main control flow of an agent such as the new case classification, new classifier reception, and data retrieval.

The security and trust layer is a crucial system component due to the sensitivity of the data. Its functionalities are access control, data marshalling, tracking of on-going data, and the evaluation of reputation and trust of agents. The agent layer is in charge of all communication and allows their abstraction from the rest of the system to allow flexibility in the underlying framework. The semantic description layer will contain the description of what the agent holds and what it is able to do.

Now we describe in more detail the layered, fully distributed, agent-based architecture that is the basis of the network on which the HealthAgents system is developed.

All sites on the system's data marts network are protected by firewalls and their connection to HealthAgents will be available in a 'de-militarised zone' (DMZ) outside of these firewalls, where agents are free to communicate. An anonymisation process is executed when porting data to the DMZ. The databases behind the firewall have not necessarily been anonymised, whereas databases in the DMZ are either link-anonymised or fully anonymised, depending on local laws or norms.

Agents in the system provide access to the functionalities a node (particular machine) on the system provides. For example, data-mart agents provide access to a database, and classifier agents provide access to the classification tools. Data and functionalities available on the system are distributed, which makes the system more robust. A cooperative network of yellow-pages agents is used to make sure agents are aware of the available resources on the system, allowing agents to submit queries based on a description of a remote agent's functionality. It is worth mentioning that classification is the main functionality available on the network, and classification agents are trained using the data source(s) from the network that meet the necessary or desired specific requirements. The trained classifiers can then be shared amongst the agents on the network to provide classification of new (perhaps private) cases at associated hospitals.

3.1. Agent Communication and the HealthAgents Ontology

The agents communicate using an RDF-based language called the HealthAgents Language (HAL). The low-level constructs used in communication are defined in the HAL ontology. Higher-level data constructs can be used by importing ontologies into the HAL messages. Also, a domain ontology describing brain tumour related concepts (HADOM) has been defined. An ontological mapping from HADOM to a relational database (the HealthAgents relational model) is provided (using D2RQ [4]), in order to match the relational database structure usually used in the hospital Data Marts. This way, the multi-agent system can fully use the flexibility of semantic web technologies while also allowing the data sites to utilise their existing human expertise for database management. Also, by providing the system semantic web querying mechanisms (such as RDQL or SPARQL), we achieve great flexibility for integration of different functionalities as the network increases.

3.2. Framework

An initial framework has been built that implements the HealthAgents architecture. The whole premise of the agent framework is to provide a way for integrating new functionalities into the system with the minimum programming effort. The framework deliberately abstracts all specific agent functionality away from its interface, and to some extent the framework allows platform independence on agent's implementation.

The framework is based on a layer design pattern – on the bottom, there is the low-level network interface, and at the top, applications. Incoming messages are filtered up through the layers until they reach the top, when domain functionality is provided. This design makes the framework independent of any agent platform – all application code is constructed on the top of the HealthAgents framework, allowing migration to other implementation platforms by re-implementation of the agent (message parsing) layer. For the first prototype, which we describe in section 6, JADE was used for the agent layer implementation, and the API abstraction is provided by a class that is implemented for the JADE agent platform using basic FIPA ACL entities [3]. Abstraction of the communication language away from the agent platform used is achieved by using HAL.

The HealthAgents framework defines an API in order that any language can be used for communication. An implementation of this API provides a parser for HAL, using Sesame [6]. Web semantic technologies are used in order to improve agents and data interoperability. Also, security and trust are considered crucial to the system, and within the framework each agent incorporates a "security guard", used to authenticate message-level security. This provides independence of the agent platform's security layer which may or may not be used.

4. Classification

HealthAgents employs machine learning methods to provide the mathematical and computational mechanisms to infer knowledge in a formal model from specific brain tumour data. HealthAgents samples brain tumour data from a training set (x_i, y_i), where x_i is an input pattern - a metabolic profile - and y_i indicates the class membership - a known pre-diagnosed brain tumour - , with the goal of learning general models from the particular samples. Such models will minimise classification errors in future unseen data and, eventually, suggest a more accurate brain tumour diagnosis.

After gathering the data to be used for the creation of the classifier, a preprocessing procedure is applied in order to make the samples of data compatible and ready for use. Once the data has been properly pre-processed, the training process takes place, where all the parameters of the mathematical model within the pattern recognition method are tuned.

In order to address the solution of such classification problems, HealthAgents is developing linear and non-linear classifiers for brain tumours employing Linear Discriminant Analysis (LDA), Support Vector Machines (SVM) and Least-Squares Support Vector Machines (LS-SVM) in combination with feature selection and feature extraction methodologies. LDA maximises the ratio between the difference of the projected means and the dispersion within the classes. Ideally, this function should be optimal when the distance between means is maximum and the inside-class dispersions are minimum. SVM are classification, non-linear function estimation, and density estimation methodologies defined in the context of statistical learning theory, kernel methods and structural risk minimisation [34]. SVM defines the optimal separating hyperplane between two classes with the maximal margin in a high dimensional space by means of the kernel trick; LS-SVM provide a reformulation of the SVM, where a linear system is solved [26].

After gathering the data to be used for the creation of the classifier, a pre-processing procedure is applied in order to make the samples of data compatible and ready for use. Once the data has been properly pre-processed, the training process takes place, where all the parameters of the mathematical model within the pattern recognition method are tuned. For each possible configuration of these parameters, an evaluation is launched (with an independent test set or, if not available, techniques like cross validation or leaving-one-out which allows efficient use of the training samples for both training and evaluation purpouses). Finally, the last stage consists of estimating the performance. This estimation is sometimes known in the literature as guessed performance and is generally carried out by using resampling techniques (typically with cross validation, although others like k-random sampling in train and/or test are often used).

The current version of the prototype already has a limited set of classifiers, but the d-DSS of HealthAgents we plan to build will have several classifiers available in the network. From the model of the system we design, clinical users will indicate which question is pertinent and will receive a selected set of classifiers that might answer that question according to the patient data submitted by the clinical node. Once the candidate classifiers are selected, the d-DSS will execute all candidates and a ranking of the classifiers for the current request will be dynamically generated, taking into account several factors like the similarity of the patient data to the data on which the classifiers were trained, the performance evaluation it achieved when created, and the usefulness and accuracy reported by the users. In the next stage, classification results are sorted by the ranking criterion. The user can then review the different results in order to compare the answers given by the classifiers, accessing the visual representation of the output.

This ranking model is a key piece of the HealthAgents system since it is critically based on the process of classifier selection. Thus, a way of measuring which are the more appropriate classifiers available in the system for each patient case to be diagnosed is needed.

Information about how well are answering the classifiers in the real environment of the d-DSS in terms of its ratio of success as well as from the users' expectations point of view and the way the classifier's answers are being used will be monitored.

In order to record the ratio of success of the classifiers, factors like the quality of the signal (in case of classifiers based on MRS) have to be taken into account. A noisy spectrum is more willing to be misclassified even by a robust classifier, thus, it would not be 'fair' to include this classification in the ratio of success of the classifiers involved in the request of classification since the signal did not cover a minimal quality criteria.

An automated method of evaluation of the signal quality for MR spectra will also be designed for the d-DSS we plan to build. When a spectrum will not overcome the quality criteria defined in [28], although the classification will be carried out by the candidate classifiers, the obtained results will not affect to the success ratio of the involved classifiers and a notification will be sent to the user indicating the poor quality of the submited spectrum.

5. Data Entry

The Data Entry for the HEALTHAGENTS system is a web front-end for the management of the HEALTHAGENTS data. HEALTHAGENTS uses a large amount of data including some types of clinical, spectroscopist, and in vivo data. Management and use of this data is crucial to the system, so that the information can be used as inputs for the classifiers, and also, visualised by the clinicians using HEALTHAGENTS.

As HEALTHAGENTS is a distributed system and will be installed in different nodes, where these nodes can have their own Data Bases, the HEALTHAGENTS Data Entry has to be "database independent" as much as possible. To avoid future problems between the relationship web front-end and the Data Base, and to ensure that the HEALTHAGENTS web front-end can be configured easily and faster to use with different databases, the decision was taken to implement it using JSF (Java Server Faces) technology. As desired, this technology supports the MVC (Model View Controller) design pattern, which divides a system into three major parts:

- View layer, with all the visual elements.
- Controller, a services layer, totally independent of presentation and exposing the business services.
- Model, a data store independent persistence layer, acting a s a bridge between the data store and business logic.

The use of JSF enables HEALTHAGENTS to use the same front-end with different databases, changing only the required layers, not all the system.

As mentioned before, some of the Data in HEALTHAGENTS has to be anonymised before being stored, so the HEALTHAGENTS system provides a set of specific applications to anonymise all required the data types. The HEALTHAGENTS data entry provides functionalities to manage information of two main types of data: Magnetic Resonance (MR) data and data from in vivo experiments. The first group includes information about Single Voxel (SV), Multi Voxel (MV) and Magnetic Resonance Images (MRI). For in vivo data, functionalities to manage RNA MicroArrays and HRMAS experiments are provided.

The Data Entry is more than a simple "data repository interface", it is a complete "data management system" that includes features to adequately manage patient data from a hospital, for example visualising spectras in a user-friendly way, viewing MRI images, producing reports, and extracting information for constructing classifiers.

Regarding security and data access policies, a complete security system based on a range of user permissions (by medical centre) is implemented in the HA data entry, making it possible, for example, to assign "edit privileges" to one user for the data from an specific centre, or just "download privileges" for the data from another centre. To ensure that no data will be lost during transfers or any possible disaster, a complete audit system is also implemented in the HEALTHAGENTS data entry. This system records all the actions done. If any action produces a change in the database content, the previous value is stored as well, so it is always possible to restore the data. The Data Entry interface is illustrated on figures 5.

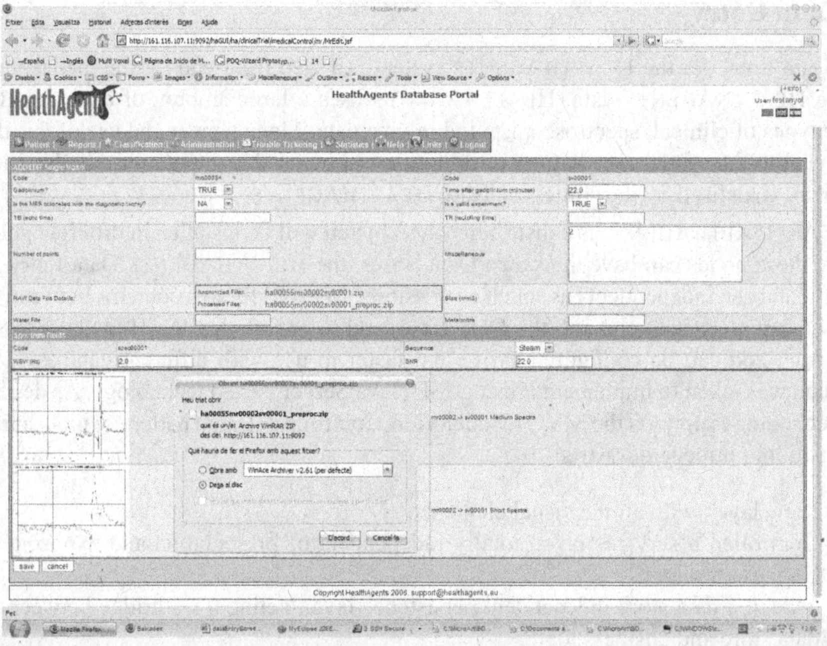

FIGURE 5. Data Entry user interface for MRS data

6. Prototype

To explore such a complex system as HealthAgents, a prototype has been created and is expected to evolve to the initial version of the system. The main purpose of the prototype is to emulate as much as possible the real necessities of the open and distributed HealthAgents environment. By now, the prototype already implements the necessary modules to create, explore and test the main functionalities of the final system. The existing centralized DSS from the Interpret project was used as a proof of concept on the development of the prototype, which enabled quick development of a specific agent framework and a semantic layer for the creation, communication and management of the agents.

New functionalities continue to be added as enhancements to the original system. Some agents were already added to the prototype: agents to provide database access, functionality to upload raw MRS data, data anonymization functionality, data pre-processing, classification (including a new GUI to show results) and finally, and evidence-based search service (ebSS). The later is a service to provide search on medical networks for information pertaining to brain tumour diagnosis, prognosis, etiology, treatment, and long-term outcome. With the fully operational integration of these services, the initial Interpret DSS was converted into a distributed DSS based on agent technology.

The first HealthAgents prototype is designed in a way to allow users to preserve their local centre policies for sharing information, whilst allowing them to benefit from the use

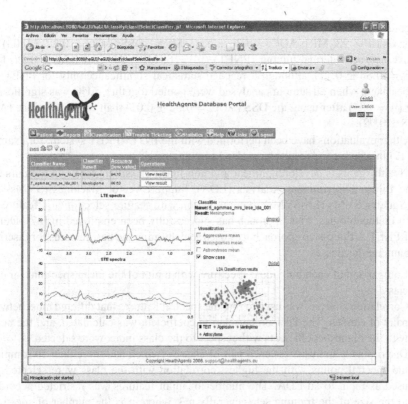

FIGURE 6. HealthAgents Prototype showing a classification result.

of a distributed data warehouse. Moreover, it will permit the design of local classifiers targeting specific patient populations. Modularity has been an important design feature, so that modules can be easily reused for the final system.

7. Evaluation

It is possible to estimate the impacts that may arise with the usage of the HealthAgents DSS by analysing the evaluation results obtained for the Interpret system. The performance of the Interpret DSS has already been extensively evaluated previously to its use in the HealthAgents project. Two different types of evaluation have been performed: usability [25], [29] and clinical.

During the DSS evaluation [27], 139 case observations were performed with MRI alone, followed by MRI and MRS combined. A single diagnosis was proposed in 116 out of 139 cases when MRI was used and in 111 out of 139 cases after MRS use. The success of the diagnosis was judged by the increase in the area under the curve (AUC) in the ROC analysis. The AUC obtained for the bilateral comparison was higher after MRS for meningiomas ($n = 20$, MRI: AUC $= 0.96 \pm 0.03$, MRI + DSS: AUC $= 0.97 \pm 0.03$), high-grade gliomas ($n = 57$, MRI: AUC $= 0.90\pm0.03$, MRI $+$ DSS: AUC $= 0.92\pm0.02$), metastases ($n = 23$, MRI: AUC $= 0.76 \pm 0.07$, MRI $+$ DSS: AUC $= 0.82 \pm 0.06$) and primitive neuroectodermal tumour (PNET) ($n = 6$, MRI: AUC $= 0.50 \pm 0.12$, MRI $+$ DSS $= 0.83 \pm 0.12$), although it reached statistical significance only for PNET. On the other hand, when all tumours analysed were pooled together, AUC was significantly higher ($n = 834$) after using the DSS (AUC $= 0.92 \pm 0.01$) than with MRI alone (AUC $= 0.88 \pm 0.02$).

Other evaluations have been performed with the INTERPRET system, for example [16], [17] in which good results have also been obtained.

HealthAgents is developing linear and non-linear classifiers for brain tumours employing Linear Discriminant Analysis (LDA), Support Vector Machines (SVMs) and Least Squares SVMs (LS-SVMs) in combination with feature selection and feature extraction methodologies. This approach has successfully been employed in [27]. During INTERPRET A three-step approach was used to determine the best features for discriminating among the classes:

1. Comparison of each individual spectrum with a plot of the mean spectrum for each class.
2. Correlation analysis was used to find the spectral features that differed most between pairs of classes. The Pearson correlation coefficient was calculated, and the points with the highest coefficients with respect to the class index were selected.
3. Discriminant analysis: for each pair of classes (which had more than 10 samples), the spectral points with the highest correlation with the class were selected and used as input to an LDA. The number of input features was restricted according to the size of the training set (generally n/3, where n is the number of spectra in the smallest group). 81 out of 91 cases (89%) were correctly classified with this approach. Additionally, the same approach has been followed during the on-going eTumour project [31].

With the aim of improving previous achievements, this background has been exploited in the HealthAgents project in order to design its first prototype, using the following framework: Java 1.4.2, Java 2 Runtime Environment (Standard Edition), Java HotSpot Client VM, Ant 1.7.0, Jade 3.4 and D2RQ 0.5. The three nodes of the Agent architecture that this first prototype is using are a Server Dell SC1425 with Red Hat Enterprise Linux for the pre-processing node, a Server Dell PowerEdge 1850 with Red Hat Enterprise Linux for the Classifier node and Workstation Dell Latitude D610 with Microsoft Windows XP for the GUI Agent.

Fig 7 illustrates the communication between GUI and Classifier Agents through the Yellow Pages Agent.

The HealthAgents Process Manager 7 tool has been built in order to monitor the operation of the system. A set of classifiers have been developed to distinguishing between certain types of tumours. One LDA example is already able to classify among three superclasses: class 1, containing the glioblastoma multiforme (gm) and metastasis (me); class 2, containing meningiomas (mm); and class 3, containing a low-glial mixture of astrocytomas grade II (a2), oligodendrogliomas (od) and oligoastrocytoma (oa).

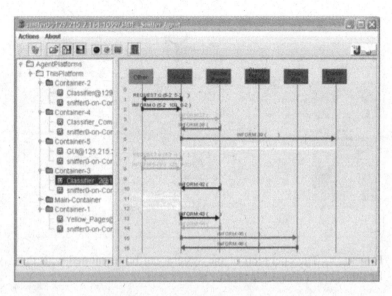

FIGURE 7. Sequence of service requests for the connection between the GUI and the classifier agents using the Yellow Pages agent.

For creating those classifiers, single voxel data collected in the Interpret project has been employed. A discriminative model has been used, adjusted using terms from Short Time Echo (STE) and Long Time Echo (LTE) and the terms in the three types were matched to single spectra points in the $[0.5, \cdots, 4.1]$ ppm range. A stepwise procedure based on the leaving-one-out evaluation of a LDA classifier has been used to obtain the subset of points more discriminant for the multi-class task. It has been observed that the combined model (LTE and STE) obtained a good accuracy ($> 90\%$) in the leaving-one-out evaluation, and a marginal improvement compared with models based on STE or LTE alone.

8. Future Work

HealthAgents is an on-going project. Here we described the state of the system half-way through its development, one year and a half after its conception. Its main design has already been defined, a first version of the Framework, the Ontology, the DataMart Schema, the Data Entry, a prototype of the d-DSS based on the INTERPRET DSS GUI, and the eBSS have already been developed, but the project needs to implement some additional parts of the system such us the classifier reputation model (briefly described in section 4), and needs to improve others like the eBSS or the GUI of the d-DSS.

The commercial version of the system is expected to be delivered at the end of 2008 under Open Source licence, for its use worldwide. New data needs also to be collected for the development of new and better classifiers, and new hospitals that might be interested in using the system are welcome and will be invited to join the network.

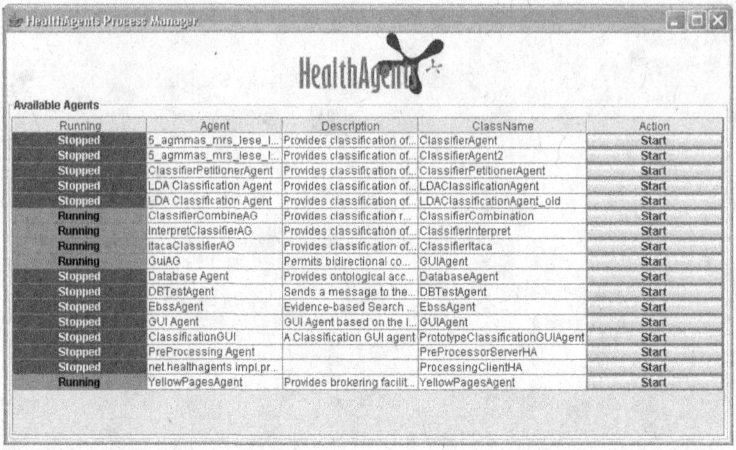

FIGURE 8. The operation of the system can be monitored with the HealthAgents Process Manager.

9. Conclusions

In vivo MRS combined with in vitro MAS and gene expression promises to improve the classification of brain tumours and yield novel biomarkers for prognosis. Considerable amounts of highly complex data are required to build reliable specific tumour classifiers and it is a challenge to collect and manage this data. HealthAgents will address this problem by building a distributed system of databases centred on the users and managed by agents. As a result, HealthAgents proposes a unique blend of state-of-the-art technologies to develop novel clinical tools for the diagnosis, management and understanding of brain tumours.

We have introduced the HealthAgents project, its objectives, and scope. HealthAgents extends the traditional scope of machine learning classification by a distributed agent-based approach, which gives the system the advantageous capability of re-training itself using aggregated sources while preserving security and patient privacy.

The HealthAgents DSS furnishes a completely new approach to brain tumour diagnosis. Its intelligent multi-agent, distributed capabilities enable the system to provide inferences based on a large range of databases. Compared to previous initiatives involving inferences from local predictions that are based on limited amounts of data and may well conflict with one another, the HealthAgents system reasoned argument among its intelligent agents is expected to produce consistent results with improved reliability and accuracy.

Although tangible results are to be produced soon, we strongly believe that the conditions are given to produce an innovative software system to help in the fight against one of the most pernicious diseases of our time: cancer.

Acknowledgement

We acknowledge all researchers involved in the project from all the partners, for their enthusiasm and cooperative work. Xavier Rafael, Roman Roset, Miguel Lurgi, Ewen Maclean, Liang Xiao, Madalina Croitoru, Miguel Esparza, Rubén Ferrer Luna, David Moner, Alexander Pérez Ruiz, Anna Barceló, Beatriz Martínez Granados, Carlos Julio Arizméndiz Pereira, Daniel Monleón, Diana Maria Sima, Ivan Olier-Caparroso, Jean Baptiste Poulet, Juan Miguel García, Juana Martín-Sitjar, Kal Natarajan, Salvador Tortajada, Sri Dasmahapatra, Teresa Delgado-Goñi, Theo Arvanitis, Xavier Vallvé, Sarah Luger and Bonnie Webber. We also thank the people that is working in the coordination and administrative side of the project, in the quality control of the software development, and the ones that are helping us in the industrialization of its results: Carol Barnwell, Simone Ristori, Corinna Carganico, Koby Tsang and Stephen Harwood.

Finally, we also acknowledge all people from outside the consortium that have expressed their support to this project, giving us their cooperation and contribution. Access to the source code for the Interpret DSS and GUI and for some preprocessing modules is gratefully acknowledged to the Interpret partners[32]. Access to the recompiled and modified INTERPRET data manipulation software is acknowledged to Guillem Mercadal.

This research has been carried out under the HealthAgents project, co-funded by the Information Society Technologies priority of the European Union Sixth Framework Programme STREP contract no.: IST-2004-27214 (2006-2008), the Centre for Innovation and Business Development of the Government of Catalonia (project ref. RDITSIND06-1-0519) and the SMEs PQE and MICROART.

References

[1] C. Arús, B. Celda, S. Dasmahapatra, D. Dupplaw, H. González-Vélez, S. van Huffel, P. Lewis, M. Lluch i Ariet, M. Mier, A. Peet, and M. Robles. On the design of a web-based decision support system for brain tumour diagnosis using distributed agents. In C. Butz, N. T. Nguyen, and Y. Takama, editors, *2006 IEEE/WIC/ACM Int Conf on Web Intelligence & Intelligent Agent Technology (WI-IAT 2006 Workshops)*, pages 208–211, Hong Kong, Dec. 2006. IEEE.

[2] S. Barton, F. Howe, A. Tomlins, S. Cudlip, J. Nicholson, B. Bell, and J. Griffiths. Comparison of in vivo 1H MRS of human brain tumours with 1H HR-MAS spectroscopy of intact biopsy samples in vitro. *Magn. Reson. Mat. Phys. Biol. Med.*, 8(2):121–128, 1999.

[3] F. Bellifemine, A. Poggi, and G. Rimassa. Jade: a fipa2000 compliant agent development environment. In *AGENTS '01: Proceedings of the fifth international conference on Autonomous agents*, pages 216–217, New York, NY, USA, 2001. ACM Press.

[4] C. Bezir. D2rq – http://sites.wiwiss.fu-berlin.de/suhl/bizer/d2rq/. web site, 2006.

[5] F. Bray, R. Sankila, J. Ferlay, and D. M. Parkin. Estimates of cancer incidence and mortality in Europe in 1995. *Eur. J. Cancer*, 38(1):99–166, 2002.

[6] J. Broekstra, A. Kampman, and F. van Harmelen. Sesame: A generic architecture for storing and querying rdf and rdf schema. In *ISWC '02: Proceedings of the First International Semantic Web Conference on The Semantic Web*, pages 54–68, London, UK, 2002. Springer-Verlag.

[7] D. Brugali and K. Sycara. Towards agent oriented application frameworks. *ACM Computing Surv.*, 32(1):21–27, 2000.

[8] G. R. Bunin, T. S. Surawicz, P. Witman, S. Preston-Martin, and J. M. B. F Davis. The descriptive epidemiology of craniopharyngioma. *J Neurosurg.*, 89(4):547–551, 1998.

[9] eTUMOUR Consortium. eTUMOUR – http://www.etumour.net/. web site, 2005.

[10] H. González-Vélez, M. Mier, M. Julià-Sapé, T. N. Arvanitis, J. M. García-Gómez, M. Robles, P. H. Lewis, S. Dasmahapatra, D. Dupplaw, A. Peet, C. Arús, B. Celda, S. V. Huffel, and M. Lluch i Ariet. Healthagents: Distributed multi-agent brain tumour diagnosis and prognosis. *Applied Intelligence*, 2007. Accepted for publication.

[11] G. Hagberg. From magnetic resonance spectroscopy to classification of tumors. a review of pattern recognition methods. *NMR Biomed.*, 11(4-5):148–156, 1998.

[12] S. Haque, D. Mital, and S. Srinivasan. Advances in biomedical informatics for the management of cancer. *Ann. N.Y. Acad. Sci.*, 980:287–297, 2002.

[13] F. A. Howe and K. S. Opstad. 1H MR spectroscopy of brain tumours and masses. *NMR Biomed.*, 16(3):123–131, 2003.

[14] M. Julià-Sapé, D. Acosta, C. Majós, A. Moreno-Torres, P. Wesseling, J. J. Acebes, J. R. Griffiths, and C. Arús. Comparison between neuroimaging classifications and histopathological diagnoses using an international multicenter brain tumor magnetic resonance imaging database. *J. Neurosurg.*, 105(1):6–14, 2006.

[15] M. Julià-Sapé, D. Acosta, M. Mier, C. Arús, D. Watson, and The INTERPRET consortium. A multi-centre, web-accessible and quality control-checked database of in vivo MR spectra of brain tumour patients. *Magn. Reson. Mat. Phys. Biol. Med.*, 19(1):22–33, 2006.

[16] M. Julià-Sapé, I. Coronel, C. Majós, M. Serrallonga, A. Candiota, M. Cos, J. Acebes, and C. Arús. A prospective study on the added value of mrs in brain tumor diagnosis. Oral presentation. ESMRMB (European Society for Magnetic Resonance in Medicine and Biology, 22nd Annual Scientific Meeting. Magnetic Resonance Materials in Physics, Biology and Medicine (MAGMA), 2005.

[17] M. Julià-Sapé, I. Coronel, M. Serrallonga, C. Majós, A. Candiota, M. Cos, O. Godino, J. Acebes, C. Aguilera, and C. Arús. The added value of mrs in brain tumor diagnosis. poster in ISMRM, Seattle, USA, 2006.

[18] C. W. Kleihues P. *Pathology and genetics of tumours of the nervous system*. International Agency for Cancer Research (IARC), 2 edition, 2000.

[19] J. V. Manjón-Herrera, M. C. Martínez-Bisbal, B. Celda, L. Martí-Bonmatí, and M. Robles. SIView 2.0: A new MR spectroscopy imaging tool. *Eur. Radiol. (Suppl.)*, 14(2):300, 2004.

[20] M. C. Martínez-Bisbal, L. Martí-Bonmatí, J. Piquer, A. Revert, P. Ferrer, J. L. Llácer, M. Piotto, O. Assemat, and B. Celda. 1H and 13C HR-MAS spectroscopy of intact biopsy samples ex vivo and in vivo. *NMR Biomed.*, 17(4):191–205, 2004.

[21] E. Merelli, G. Armano, N. Cannata, F. Corradini, M. d Inverno, A. Doms, P. Lord, A. Martin, L. Milanesi, S. Möller, M. Schroeder, , and M. Luck. Agents in bioinformatics, computational and systems biology. *Brief. Bioinform.*, 2006. In press.

[22] E. Merelli and F. Corradini. BioAgent – http://www.bioagent.org. web site, 2005.

[23] P. Mischel, T. Cloughesy, and S. Nelson. DNA-microarray analysis of brain cancer: molecular classification for therapy. *Nature Rev. Neuroscience*, 5:782–792, 2004.

[24] C. L. Nutt, D. R. Mani, R. A. Betensky, P. Tamayo, J. G. Cairncross, C. Ladd, U. Pohl, C. Hartmann, M. E. McLaughlin, T. T. Batchelor, P. M. Black, A. von Deimling, S. L. Pomeroy, T. R. Golub, and D. N. Louis. Gene expression-based classification of malignant gliomas correlates better with survival than histological classification. *Cancer Res.*, 63:1602–1607, 2003.

[25] J. U. Rosemary. Focussing user studies: Requirements capture for a decision support tool.

[26] J. A. K. Suykens and J. Vandewalle. Least squares support vector machine classifiers. *Neural Processing Letters*, 9(3):293–300, 1999.

[27] A. R. Tate, Underwood, Acosta, Juli-Sap, Majs, Moreno-Torres, Howe, van der Graaf, Lefournier, Murphy, Loosemore, Ladroue, Wesseling, L. Bosson, Cabaas, Simonetti, Gajewicz, Calvar, Capdevila, Wilkins, Bell, Rmy, Heerschap, Watson, Griffiths, and C. Arús. Development of a decision support system for diagnosis and grading of brain tumours using in vivo magnetic resonance single voxel spectra. *NMR Biomed.*, 19(4):411–434, 2006.

[28] A. R. Tate, J. Underwood, D. M. Acosta, M. Julià-Sapé, C. Majós, A. Moreno-Torres, F. A. Howe, M. van der Graaf, V. Lefournier, M. M. Murphy, A. Loosemore, C. Ladroue, P. Wesseling, J. L. Bosson, M. E. C. nas, A. W. Simonetti, W. Gajewicz, J. Calvar, A. Capdevila, P. R. Wilkins, B. A. Bell, C. Rémy, A. Heerschap, D. Watson, J. R. Griffiths, and C. Arús. Development of a decision support system for diagnosis and grading of brain tumours using in vivo magnetic resonance single voxel spectra. *NMR Biomed.*, 19(4):411–434, 2006.

[29] A. R. Tate, J. Underwood, C. Ladroue, R. Luckin, and J. R. Griffiths. Visualisation of multidimensional data for medical decision support. In *AIME '01: Proceedings of the 8th Conference on AI in Medicine in Europe*, pages 55–58, London, UK, 2001. Springer-Verlag.

[30] The HealthAgents Consortium. HealthAgents – http://www.healthagents.net. web site, 2006-2008. Funded by the IST priority of the EU's FP6 (Contract no.: IST-2004-27214).

[31] S. Tortajada, J. M. García-Gómez, C. Vidal, C. Arús, M. Julià-Sapé, A. Moreno, and M. Robles. Improved classification by pattern recognition of brain tumours combining long and short echo time 1H-MR spectra. In *23rd Annual ESMRMB Meeting*. European Society of Magnetic Resonance for Medicine and Biology, 2006.

[32] Universitat Autònoma de Barcelona. INTERPRET project – http://azizu.uab.es/INTERPRET/. web site, 2005.

[33] University of Southampton. AgentLink – http://www.agentlink.org/. web site, 2005.

[34] V. N. Vapnik. *The Nature of Statistical Learning Theory*. Statistics for Engineering and Information Science. Springer-Verlag, New York, 2 edition, 1999.

[35] J. T. Yao. Design of web-based support systems. In *8th Int Conf on Computer Science and Informatics*, pages 349–352, Salt Lake City, USA, July 2005. CSI.

Magí Lluch-Ariet, Francesc Estanyol and Mariola Mier
MicroArt, SL
Parc Cientfic de Barcèlona
Baldiri Reixac, 4-6
08028 Barcelona
Catalonia
www.microart.eu
e-mail: info@microart.eu

Carla Delgado
University of Edinburgh and MicroArt, SL

Horacio González–Vélez and Tiphaine Dalmas
University of Edinburgh

Montserrat Robles, Carlos Sáez and Javier Vicente
Instituto de Aplicaciones de las TIC Avanzadas

Sabine Van Huffel and Jan Luts
Katholieke Universiteit Leuven

Carles Arús, Ana Paula Candiota Silveira and Margarida Julià–Sapé
Universitat Autònoma de Barcelona

Andrew Peet, Alex Gibb and Yu Sun
University of Birmingham

Bernardo Celda and Maria Carmen Martínez Bisbal
Universitat de Valencia and CIBER-BBN Instituto Salud Carlos III

Giulia Valsecchi
Pharma Quality Europe

David Dupplaw, Bo Hu and Paul Lewis
University of Southampton

Whitestein Series in Software Agent Technologies, 25–44
© 2007 Birkhäuser Verlag Basel/Switzerland

SAPHIRE: A Multi-Agent System for Remote Healthcare Monitoring through Computerized Clinical Guidelines

Gokce B. Laleci, Asuman Dogac, Mehmet Olduz, Ibrahim Tasyurt, Mustafa Yuksel and Alper Okcan

Abstract. Due to increasing percentage of graying population and patients with chronic diseases, the world is facing serious problems for serving high quality healthcare services to citizens at a reasonable costs. In this paper, we are providing a Clininical Desicion Support system for remote monitoring of patients at their homes, and at the hospital to decrease the load of medical practitioners and also healthcare costs. As the expert knowledge required to build the clinical decision support system, Clinical Guidelines are exploited. Examining the reasons of failure for adoption of clinical guidelines by healthcare institutes, we have realized that necessary measures should be taken in order to establish a semantic interoperability environment to be able to communicate with various heterogenous clinical systems. In this paper these requirements are detailed and a semantic infrastructure to enable easy deployment and execution of clinical guidelines in heterogenous healthcare enviroments is presented. Due to the nature of the problem which necessitates having many autonomous entities dealing with heterogenous distributed resources, we have built the system as a Multi-Agent System. The architecture described in this paper is realized within the scope of IST-27074 SAPHIRE project.

1. Introduction

The World is facing problems to provide high quality healthcare services at a reasonable cost to the citizens due to the increasing percentage of graying population. According to a study performed by United Nations, by 2050, 22 percent of

This work is supported by the European Commission through IST-27074 SAPHIRE project and in part by the Scientific and Technical Research Council of Turkey, Project No: EEEAG 105E133.

the World's population, nearly 2 billion people, will be 60 and older. With the demographic change, the prevalence of chronic conditions such as chronic respiratory and vessel diseases increases: the percentage of elderly at 60s and older having at least one chronic disease is more than 60 [1]. The solution to decrease both the cost of healthcare services and also the load of medical practitioners requires a dramatic change in the way future healthcare services are provided. The expected necessary changes are: moving from reactive to preventive medicine, concentrating on the long term care rather than only acute care, citizen centered care rather than hospital centered care, including remote care delivery mechanisms where the citizen is taking a bigger role in his/her treatment and lifestyle management. All of these necessitate technologies for long term monitoring of the patients both in hospital and home settings.

Enabling underlying infrastructures such as wireless medical sensor devices, wearable medical systems integrating sensors on body-worn platforms like wrist-worn devices or biomedical clothes are offering pervasive solutions for continuous health status monitoring through non-invasive biomedical, biochemical and physical measurements. Remote monitoring systems typically collect these patient readings and then transmit them to a remote server for storage and later examination by healthcare professionals. Once available on the server, the readings can be used in numerous ways by home health agencies, by clinicians, by physicians, and by informal care providers. However remote healthcare monitoring systems will be exploited to their full potential when the analysis is also performed automatically through clinical decision support systems fed by expert knowledge. Clinical practice guidelines constitutes the most suitable source of information for building such clinical decision support systems.

Clinical practice guidelines are the systematically developed statements designed to assist practitioners to make decisions about appropriate medical problems. They aim to reduce inter-practice variations and cost of medical services, improve quality of care and standardize clinical procedures [2]. In order to be able to share clinical guidelines and manage their enforcement through computerized systems, a number of machine processable models of Clinical Guidelines have been proposed such as GLIF [3], ASBRU [4], ARDEN [5] and EON [6]. Based on these machine processable guideline definitions, a number of clinical decision support systems have been built such as GLEE [7], GLARE [8] and DeGel [9].

Despite the benefits of clinical guidelines, and also although we have such machine processable models and clinical decision support systems for execution them, it has been a well accepted fact that wide adoption computerized clinical practice guidelines has yet to be achieved even within a single healthcare institute. This is because of the difficulty of integration of clinical decision support systems with the already existing clinical workflow systems run by healthcare institutes: for this the clinical decision support system needs to communicate with various heterogeneous clinical applications run by the healthcare institute [10, 11]. Especially in the case of long term and remote monitoring of the patients, the clinical decision support systems need to communicate with many different information sources:

medical devices, several electronic healthcare record systems, and the decisions need to affect the processes held at disparate care providers such as homecare, emergency centers, primary and secondary care, and rehabilitation centers. Hence we definitely need robust clinical guideline execution systems that can cope with semantic and technical integration problems with disparate healthcare information systems.

In this paper, the SAPHIRE project will be introduced which provides a Multi-Agent system for the monitoring of chronic diseases both at hospital and also in home environments based on a semantic infrastructure. The system is capable of deploying and executing clinical guidelines in a care environment including many disparate care providers having heterogeneous information systems. In Section 2, the challenges and requirements of deploying and executing a clinical guideline execution infrastructure for remote monitoring of patients in a heterogeneous care environment will be detailed. In Section 3, the SAPHIRE Multi-Agent System that addresses these challenges through an enabling semantic interoperability environment will be introduced. Finally Section 4 will conclude the paper, discussing the current status and future challenges.

2. The requirements for seamless execution of Clinical Guidelines for long term healthcare monitoring

In order to guarantee successful execution of clinical decision support systems for long term monitoring of patients based on clinical practice guidelines, the integration, more importantly interoperability, with the following external interfaces should be assured:

- *Accessing vital signs of the patient:* In order to be able to monitor the patient's current condition, the clinical decision support systems need to access the vital signs of the patient measured by wireless medical sensors and body-worn platforms. Currently there are many biomedical sensors devices available, and active research is going on for body worn platforms initial products of which will be soon in the market. The clinical decision support systems should be able to communicate with heterogeneous medical devices supplied by various different vendors. We have two interoperability problems to access the vital signs measured by these devices: the first one is the technical interoperability problem to access the vital signs physically: there may be different protocols implemented by different medical device vendors.

  In SAPHIRE architecture we are addressing the technical level interoperability problem by exposing the sensor data through Web Services. The sensor data is gathered through Bluetooth from wireless sensor devices to a gateway computer where they are exposed as Web services. By exposing the sensor data as Web services, a platform independent way of accessing the vital signs measured by sensor devices is achieved.

The second interoperability challenge that should be addressed is content level interoperability problem: After accessing the sensor data through Web services, the content received should be processable and interpretable by the receiving application, the clinical decision support system in our case. However, the data coming from the wireless medical sensors are either in proprietary format (for example, for electrocardiogram data, Philips XML ECG Data Format) or when it conforms to a standard, this still does not solve the interoperability problem since there are very many standards (again for electrocardiogram data, the available standards include: SCP-ECG [12], US Food and Drug Administration FDA/HL7 Annotated ECG [13], I-Med [14] and ecgML[15]).

There is also a very important interoperability initiative for the interoperability of the data coming from medical devices: the IEEE 11073 Standards Family[16] which aims to enable functional and semantic ad-hoc interoperability. For this purpose, the IEEE 11073 proposes an Object-oriented modeling of function and application area, the "Domain Information Model" (DIM). Through the DIM it is possible to define and represent devices, functionalities, measurement data, calibrations, alert information and so on. On top of the DIM, it provides standardized codes for naming all information elements in the DIM such as medical devices and device systems, units of measurements through the "Nomenclature" and "Data Dictionary". IEEE 11073 assumes that all device vendors to adopt this DIM to represent sensor data to achieve interoperability. However for the time being the vendors still using proprietary formats or different standards can not be ignored.

In our architecture we provide a translation wizard, through which the translation of proprietary XML schemas of sensor data to the IEEE 11073 format can be easily defined graphically enabling the user to define Javascripts taking the pieces of input XSD schema. This translation definition is used to transform the data instances automatically to one another. In this way it is possible to have all the sensor data in IEEE 11073 format in SAPHIRE Gateway computer to be exposed as Web services.

- *Accessing Electronic Healthcare Records of the Patient:* The gathered vital signs of the patient can only be assessed correctly when consolidated with the Electronic Healthcare Records (EHRs) of the patient. The evaluation of the vital signs should be "personalized" for each patient, based on their past illnesses, active problems, family histories, allergies and adverse reactions. In addition to this, the clinical decision support system executing clinical guidelines needs to know the previous medical history of the patient to follow the correct branch for the medication or operation recommendations to be presented to the medical staff: for example the first line medication to be applied to a patient who may be suffering from myocardial infarction varies based on his/her medical history: it is not appropriate to recommend a B-blocker if the patient previously suffered from bronchial spasm or asthma. To be able assess these, the clinical guideline execution environment needs to access the

Electronic Healthcare Records of the Patient where ever they are. However there is a challenge to be addressed here: Patient medical records that the clinical decision support system need to process are usually physically dispersed in disparate medical institutions which usually do not interoperate with each other. First of all the Clinical Decision support system needs to discover these records, and then needs to seamlessly access the records to process them. One of the prominent initiatives for sharing EHRs is the Integrating Healthcare Enterprise (IHE). IHE, through the Cross Enterprise Document Sharing Integration Profile (XDS) [17], enables a number of healthcare delivery organizations to share clinical records. This profile has received considerable attention and appeared in the National eHealth System blueprints of Canada, USA, Italy, Norway and France.

In the IHE XDS Profile, healthcare enterprises that agree to work together for clinical document sharing are called a "Clinical Affinity Domain". Such institutes agree on a common set of policies such as how the patients are identified, the access is controlled, and the common set of coding terms to represent the metadata of the documents.

In each affinity domain there are a number of "Document Repositories"; the healthcare institutes store the medical documents of the patients to these repositories in a transparent, secure, reliable and persistent way. There is a "Document Registry" which is responsible for storing information about those documents so that the documents of interest for the care of a patient may be easily found, selected and retrieved irrespective of the repository where they are actually stored. The document repositories register the documents along with a set of metadata to the Document Registry. Whenever a "DocumentConsumer" wishes to locate a specific document of a patient, the "Query Document" transaction is issued along with the specified query criteria, and as a response a list of document entries that contain metadata found to meet the specified criteria is returned including the locations and identifier of each corresponding document in one or more Document Repositories. Using these document identifiers and the Document Repository URI's, the "Retrieve Document" transaction is issued to get the document content.

The SAPHIRE multi-agent system that facilitates the execution of the clinical decision support system uses this IHE Profile to locate and access the records of the patients which will be detailed in Section 3.

The Electronic Healthcare Records accessed should be machine processable so that the content can be interpreted to retrieve the necessary piece of the EHR required by the clinical guideline definition. For this purpose in SAPHIRE architecture, the EHR documents are represented as the HL7 Clinical Document Architecture (CDA) [18] documents. The HL7 CDA is a document markup standard that specifies the structure and semantics of "clinical documents" for the purpose of exchange. CDA documents are encoded in Extensible Markup Language (XML) and they derive their machine processable meaning from the HL7 Reference Information Model (RIM) [19] and use the HL7 Version 3 Data Types. In the SAPHIRE architecture, both the "Sections" and "Document Entries" are annotated with coded terms of medical terminologies and ontologies such as LOINC [20], SNOMED [21] and ICD-10 [22] so that the clinical guideline execution environment can process the information contained in the EHR of the patient. However it should be noted that, in the clinical guideline definition the clinical information requested may have been represented through a code in a different medical terminology from the one that has been used in the CDA document, in this case, the "Ontology Agent" of SAPHIRE multi-agent system is contacted to handle the mediation between different coding standards.

- *Accessing the Clinical Workflow systems executed at Healthcare Institutes:* While the clinical decision support system is executing the Clinical Guideline Definition, it is needed to interact with several modules of the clinical workflow executed at the healthcare institutions. For example, if the clinical decision support system recommends to prescribe a B-Blocker to a patient, this medication recommendation should be reflected to the underlying clinical workflow, otherwise the clinical decision support system and the clinical workflow run in parallel without any interaction with each other, the activities are not synchronized with each other.

These kind of problems hamper the use of clinical decision support systems to their full potential. For this kind of interactions like medication, procedure or lab orders, there needs to be an interface provided by the underlying hospital information system executing the clinical workflow. However most of the hospital information systems are proprietary, which makes the deployment of clinical decision support systems to healthcare institutes difficult. Integration with each of such hospital information system is costly; there needs to be a mechanism that enables interoperability for accessing these proprietary systems to avoid manual integration efforts.

In SAPHIRE, we are proposing to solve this problem by exposing the functionalities provided by Healthcare Institutions as Web Services, and publishing these Web services to Service registries by annotating them with ontologies reflecting their functionality. This will allow us to automatically deploying the clinical decision support systems executing clinical guidelines automatically. Web services have already started to be adopted by the Healthcare Industry as a solution to technical interoperability problem. The Dutch national infrastructure for healthcare messaging is implemented by wrapping HL7v3 messages as Web services [23].

3. The SAPHIRE Multi-Agent System

The SAPHIRE Clinical Decision Support System that is responsible for deploying and executing Clinical Guidelines is a multi-agent system composed of a number of collaborating agents. An overview of the subcomponents and their interaction

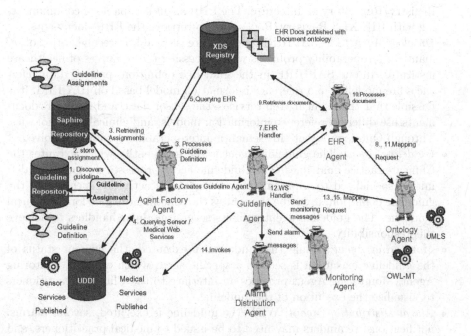

FIGURE 1. The SAPHIRE Multi-Agent System

is depicted in Figure 1. The system is implemented as a multiagent system, since as a result of conceptual design phase we have realized that in order to deploy and execute the clinical guidelines in a heterogeneous distributed environment, there should be a number of autonomous components that should be communicating with each other in a reactive manner, and some of these components should be instantiated and eliminated dynamically based on the demand.

The roles of each SAPHIRE Agent can be introduced as follows:

- *Agent Factory Agent*: The Agent Factory Agent is mainly responsible for specializing the Guideline definition to a patient, and creating the Guideline Agent which will execute the clinical guideline. It discovers the real implementations of the medical services exposing hospital information system functionalities and sensor services and the document identifiers of the EHR documents of the patients, so that the guideline definition becomes ready to be executed.

- *EHR Agent*: In the SAPHIRE architecture the EHR agent functions as the gateway to access and extract clinical data from the Electronic Healthcare records of the patient. EHR Agent is modelled as a separate agent, to abstract the access to EHR from other agents. Currently in the SAPHIRE architecture the main mechanism for sharing EHR documents is IHE XDS

Registry/Repository architecture. The EHR agent is capable of communicating with IHE XDS Registry/Repository to retrieve the EHR documents.

- *Ontology Agent*: The SAPHIRE architecture is capable of reconciliation of semantic interoperability problems while accessing the resources of healthcare institutes. In the SAPHIRE in the guideline definition, patient data references are modelled in a reference information model based on HL7 RIM. It is possible that the medical Web services, the sensor data, and the EHR documents use different reference information models, and clinical terminologies. Through Ontology Agent this semantic interoperability problem is solved.

- *Guideline Agent*: The guideline agent is the main entity which executes the Clinical practice guidelines. The Guideline agent processes the guideline definition specialized to a patient and executes the activities specified in the guideline definition. It can be thought as the enactment engine for the clinical guideline. The guideline agent exploits several modular handlers to achieve this responsibility.

- *Monitoring Agent*: While the guideline is executed, the current status of the guideline execution is sent to a specific agent which we call Monitoring Agent. Monitoring Agent provides an interface to the Clinical Practitioners to visualize the execution of the guideline.

- *Alarm Distribution Agent*: While the guideline is executed, several alarms, notifications, reminders may need to be issued to medical practitioners, and when necessary to the patient relatives. In such cases the alarm message and the role to whom the message should be delivered is informed to an agent, the Alarm Distribution Agent, which is specifically designated to distribute these messages to the necessary recipients in the most efficient and reliable way.

For implementing the SAPHIRE Multi-Agent system we have utilized the JADE [24] agent development platform. In the following sections the functionalities of the SAPHIRE Agents will be detailed.

3.1. EHR Agent

As presented in section 2, accessing the Electronic Healthcare Records of the patient is an indispensable requirement for automatic remote monitoring of the patient. However the EHR's of a patient may be stored separately in each healthcare institute s/he has been previously hospitalized. In SAPHIRE Architecture, the healthcare institutes that cooperate for the care of a patient are grouped as Clinical Affinity domains. These clinical affinity domains may have agreed on different platforms for sharing the EHRs of the patient that are not interoperable with each other. This is in fact a real life situation: in U.K as the national health infrastructure, a central architecture called SPINE [25] will be used for sharing medical summaries of patients, while in Canada, an IHE-XDS based infrastructure is being built for the same purpose [26]. To abstract the access to the EHR from the Clinical Guideline Execution Environment, we have created a dedicated agent, the EHR agent for each such affinity domain. EHR agent can be thought as a gateway for locating and accessing EHRs of the patients. Each EHR agent is specialized in the platform agreed in that affinity domain for sharing EHRs. When a request for discovering and requesting an EHR document is received by an EHR agent, the EHR agent both tries to locate the EHR document within its affinity domain, through the methodology agreed by the clinical affinity domain such as IHE-XDS, and also forwards the request to the EHR agents of the other clinical affinity domains. In this way, the EHR documents will be available to the requesting entity, although heterogeneous systems are used by different affinity domains. In our architecture, we have implemented EHR agents accessing the IHE-XDS EHR Registry/Repositories: When a specific EHR of a specific patient is saught, an EHR Discovery message is sent to the EHR Agent. In this message, the patient identifier is presented and the document type metadata is specified with "LOINC Document Type Codes" such as "11450-4" for "Active Problems". Using this metadata, and the patient identifier, a "QueryDocument" transaction is issued to the XDS Registry, and as a response a set of Document Identifiers pointing to document stored in EHR Repositories is presented. These document identifiers are used to access the document content from the Repositories by issuing a "RetrieveDocument" transaction.

Apart from locating and retrieving EHR documents, EHR agents also serve another important feature: retrieving a specific piece of information from the EHR content. The EHR content standard agreed by each clinical affinity domain may be different, however the EHR agent of that domain, is capable of processing the document format agreed and extract the requested piece of information in the format requested by the Clinical guideline execution environment. As presented in section 2, in our architecture, we are using HL7 CDA documents as EHR documents, and in our implementation, we have implemented an EHR agent that is capable of processing the CDA document, locate the requested piece of information among the CDA Entries, and present it to the requesting entity.

In the EHR access request sent to the EHR Agent, the semantics of the piece of information requested is also specified with coded terms. For example, the Clinical Guideline Execution Environment is in need of discovering whether the patient has previously experienced "asthma". In the request sent to the EHR agent, besides the document type code for "Past illnesses", the coded term representing "asthma" is also specified for example as "C0004096" in UMLS medical terminology. In the CDA document all the entries are also annotated with coded terms, however another code from a different terminology may have been used for identifying the same entry in the CDA document which could be the "J45" term from ICD-10 terminology. To solve this interoperability problem, the EHR agent consults to the Ontology agent, and receives an answer to its translation request. In this way although different medical terminologies may have been used, the requested part of the EHR can be extracted from the whole EHR document.

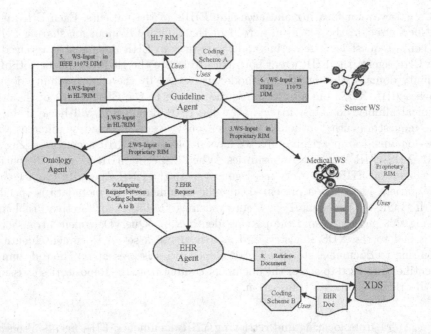

FIGURE 2. The SAPHIRE Ontology Agent

3.2. Ontology Agent

The Ontology Agent in SAPHIRE Architecture is responsible for handling the semantic mediation of the clinical content used in SAPHIRE Architecture. It is used for the following purposes as presented in Figure 2:

- *Mapping the parameters of Medical Web Services*: In the SAPHIRE Architecture, the guideline execution environment uses a reference information model based on HL7 RIM subset to represent the clinical information. However, it is a fact that several other standards or even propriety formats may be used by the healthcare institutes to represent clinical information. The guideline execution environment needs to communicate with the hospital information systems to reflect the results of guideline execution. For example, the guideline execution can result with a proposal of prescription of a medication to the patient; in this case this information may need to be stored to the hospital information system to affect the clinical workflow. In SAPHIRE architecture, these kinds of interactions are handled through the Web services exposed by the healthcare institutes. However it is natural that the parameters of these Web services are conforming to the messaging and content standards used within the hospital, not to the one used in the guideline execution environment. Whenever the Guideline Agent needs to invoke a Medical Web Service, it consults with the Ontology Agent and the input parameters are automatically mediated to the messaging and content standards used by the hospital. The same mechanism is used for mapping the output parameters.

- *Mapping the parameters of Sensor Web Services*: In the SAPHIRE Architecture, the guideline execution environment represents the sensor data to be used in guideline execution in the same reference information model based on HL7 RIM. Currently in our architecture the sensor data will be exposed as Web services which represent the data in IEEE 11073 DIM. Whenever a data is received form a Sensor Web Service, the Guideline Agent consults with the Ontology Agent to mediate the sensor data to the reference information model used in the guideline execution environment.
- *Mapping the content of the Electronic Healthcare Records of the Patient*: In the SAPHIRE architecture the Electronic Healthcare Records of the patients are represented as HL7 CDA documents. In HL7 CDA, the document sections and entities can be coded with coded terms from different coding schemes. In SAPHIRE, in the guideline definition model the EHR data can also be annotated with concepts from ontologies or coding schemes. Whenever different coding scheme standards are used, the Ontology Agent is consulted for mediation. Since the Guideline Agent cooperates with the EHR Agent whenever an EHR content is necessary, the mediation request to Ontology Agent is sent by the EHR Agent.

The Ontology Agent is compliant with the FIPA Ontology Service Specifications [27]. According to FIPA Specification an Ontology Agent is an agent that provides access to one or more ontology servers and which provide ontology services to an agent community. The Ontology Agent (OA) is responsible for the one or some of these services:

- maintain (for example, register with the DF, upload, download, and modify) a set of public ontologies,
- translate expressions between different ontologies and/or different content languages,
- respond to query for relationships between terms or between ontologies,

The FIPA Specification deals with a standard way to serve the ontology services; it does not mandate any mechanism on how to map the ontologies to one another. As well as all the other agents, the OA registers its service with the Directory Facilitator (DF) and it also registers the list of maintained ontologies and their translation capabilities in order to allow agents to query the DF for the specific OA that manages a specific ontology. Being compliant with the FIPA Ontology Service Specification necessitates the Ontology Agent to be able to accept and respond to the ontology service requests in FIPA-Ontol-Service-Ontology ontology. An example translation request and response is presented in Figure 3.

As presented the FIPA Ontology Service Specification does not deal with how the mapping is facilitated. In the SAPHIRE Architecture, the mapping is facilitated through three different mediation mechanisms (Figure 2):

An example translation request	An example response to a translation request
(request	(inform
:sender	:sender
(agent-identifier	(agent-identifier
:name client-agent@foo.com	:name ontology-agent@foo.com
:addresses (sequence iiop://foo/acc))	:addresses (sequence iiop://foo.com/acc))
:receiver (set	:receiver (set
(agent-identifier	(agent-identifier
:name ontology-agent@foo.com	:name client-agent@foo.com
:addresses (sequence iiop://foo.com/acc)))	:addresses (sequence iiop://foo.com/acc)))
:protocol FIPA-Request	:language FIPA-SL2
:language FIPA-SL2	:ontology (set FIPA-Ontol-Service-Ontology)
:ontology FIPA-Ontol-Service-Ontology	:content
:content	(= (iota ?i
(action	(result
(agent-identifier	(action
:name ontology-agent@foo.co	(agent-identifier
:addresses (sequence iiop://foo.com/acc))	:name ontology-agent@foo.com
(translate (**C0262926**))	:addresses (sequence iiop://foo.com/acc))
(translation-description	(translation-description
:from UMLSDocTypeOntology	:from UMLSDocTypeOntology
:to LOINCDocTypeOntology)))	:to LOINCDocTypeOntology))) ?i))
:reply-with translation-query-1123234)	(**11348-0**))
	:in-reply-to translation-query-1123234)

FIGURE 3. An example translation request and response

- *Mapping the parameters of Medical Web Services*: In one of our previous projects, Artemis [28], we have developed an OWL Ontology Mapping Tool, the OWLmt [29], to mediate the input and output parameters of medical Web services between different standards. The SAPHIRE Ontology Agent handles such mapping requests through the OWLmt tool. The OWLmt tool provides a graphical interface to define the mapping patterns between OWL ontologies in different structures but with an overlapping content. This mapping definition is used to automatically translate ontology instances to one another. In SAPHIRE, the schemas of Web service messages, and the schema of the Reference Information Model used by the clinical guideline execution environment are lifted to metamodel level and represented as OWL ontologies. Then through the OWLmt GUI, the mapping relationships between them is defined graphically once, which will be used by the OWLmt Mapping engine to mediate the Web service parameters to the reference information model understood by the clinical guideline execution environment. For the details of the OWLmt tool, please refer to [29], where detailed examples of mapping definitions from medical domain are presented.

- *Mapping the terminologies used in Clinical Document Content*: The SAPHIRE Ontology Agent handles such requests through a Web service exposing the functionalities of the UMLS Knowledge Source Server [30] . The UMLS Metathesaurus contains information about biomedical concepts and terms from many controlled vocabularies and classifications used in patient records, administrative health data, bibliographic and full-text databases, and expert system. These are referred to as the "source vocabularies" of the Metathesaurus. The Metathesaurus reflects and preserves the meanings, concept names, and relationships from its source vocabularies. The UMLS Knowledge Sources are also downloadable as databases in UMLS Site. In SAPHIRE architecture, we have implemented a Web service that queries the local UMLS database, for finding the synonyms of clinical terms. synonym terms in ICD10, LOINC and SNOMED CT if there are any.

- *Mapping the parameters of Sensor Web Services*: As presented in Section 2 the Sensor data is exposed as Web services in IEEE 11073 DIM. However this information in DIM, should be translated to HL7 RIM which is used by the clinical guideline execution environment. The IEEE 11073 Standards family names this level as "Observation Reporting Interface", and provides guidelines to map the IEEE 11073 DIM to the HL7 observation reporting messages, segments, and fields. The SAPHIRE Ontology agent implements these guidelines to handle this mediation.

3.3. Agent Factory Agent

In the SAPHIRE Architecture the agent that is responsible for leading the deploying a generic clinical guideline definition to a specific patient in a healthcare institution is the Agent Factory Agent.

In SAPHIRE, we have selected GLIF (Guide Line Interchange Format) [3] as the computer interpretable model of clinical guidelines. However GLIF was originally developed as a standard representation model for sharing guidelines among different healthcare institutes, rather than automatically deploying clinical guidelines to a healthcare institute. For example, when clinical information is needed to be retrieved, in the original GLIF, only "EHR" or "Doctor" can be represented as the source of clinical information. It is apparent that with this amount of information it is not possible to use it as an executable model of clinical guidelines. This necessity as the "requirement for an implementable representation" is also specified in GLIF's latest specification as a future work.

Within the scope of SAPHIRE project, we have extended the original GLIF model, and semantically annotated the external interfaces of the guideline execution environment with EHR systems, Medical sensor devices and Healthcare Information Systems so that the required resources such as EHR documents can be dynamically discovered in the deployment phase. We have extended the model so that:

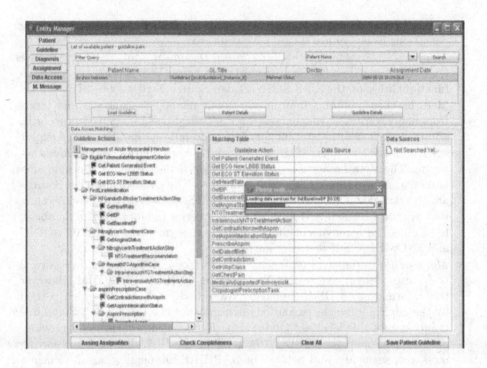

FIGURE 4. The SAPHIRE Agent Factory GUI

- the functionality of the medical procedures to be interacted can be specified through ontologies.
- both the type of the EHR document sought, and also the type of the piece of information looked for in the EHR document can be specified through ontologies or medical terminologies.
- the kind of vital signs can be specified through a coded term in reference to a terminology identifying medical measurements such as IEEE 11073 Nomenclature.

The details of this extension can be found in [31, 32].

The Agent Factory Agent processes the clinical guideline definitions represented in our extended model, and based on the semantic annotations of the external resources, discovers the instances of the specified resources that are relevant for our specific patient. This process can be summarized as follows:

- In SAPHIRE architecture, the medical Web services exposing functionalities of healthcare information systems, and also the sensor Web services exposing the sensor data retrieved from wireless medical sensor devices are published to a UDDI registry by annotating them with their functionality semantics. Whenever the Agent Factory encounters a reference to a medical procedure,

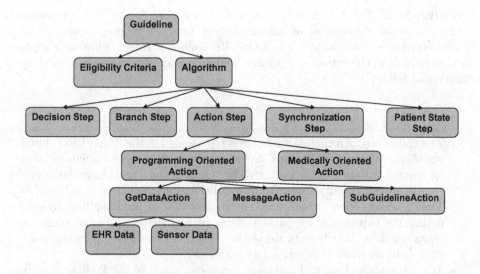

FIGURE 5. The SAPHIRE Guideline Agent Handlers

it locates the medical procedures from UDDI service registries by their functionality which has been specified in the extended GLIF model.

- Whenever the Agent Factory encounters a reference to a clinical data of patient to be retrieved from an EHR document, it sends a message to the EHR agent presenting the Document type, and Entry type semantics presented in the extended GLIF model. As a response a set of document identifiers are received pointing to relevant EHR documents.

In addition to that, in the extended GLIF model, we have also reserved slots for storing the pointers to the discovered resources, for example, document identifiers in EHR repositories, the WSDL and OWL-S files of Web services. As a result of the deployment phase briefly presented, the agent factory specializes the generic guideline definition to a patient by filling in these slots.

Whenever the clinical guideline is wished to be executed for remote monitoring of a specific patient, the Agent Factory Agent instantiates a dedicated Guideline Agent for a specific guideline patient pair. In addition to this, the Agent Factory Agent informs the Monitoring Agent, about this instantiation, so that the execution of the remote monitoring process can be traced by clinical practitioners.

3.4. Guideline Agent

Guideline agent is the leading agent that coordinates the execution of the clinical guideline definition for remote monitoring of the patients. SAPHIRE Guideline agent is capable of processing any guideline definition represented in the extended GLIF model, and execute the guideline in cooperation with the other entities of

SAPHIRE Multi-Agent System. As presented in Figure 5, the guideline definition is composed of a number of building blocks, for each building block we have
implemented modular handlers. The SAPHIRE Guideline Agent behavior is implemented to process the extended guideline definition and instantiate these modular
handlers as follows:

- The main body of a clinical guideline is represented in the "Algorithm" building block. "Patient State steps" are not executable, can be though as labels
  for current situation of the patient. The "Branch and Synchronization Steps"
  coordinate the execution of serial or parallel execution of algorithm branches.
  The "Decision Steps" coordinate the control flow of the guideline, by evaluating the expressions on patient state. In SAPHIRE, the expressions are
  represented as Java Scripts using the content of the EHR documents and
  vital signs received from sensors as parameters.
- The "Medically Oriented Actions" represent the medical Web services in
  the extended GLIF definition. The guideline agent extracts the WSDL of
  the Web service from the guideline definition specialized to a patient by the
  Agent Factory Agent. The Guideline agent prepares the input parameters in
  HL7 RIM, since GLIF uses this RIM for representing clinical data. While the
  Web services are discovered from the UDDI registry by the Agent Factory,
  the OWL-S files of the Web services are also retrieved and saved to the
  specialized guideline definition. Using this OWL-S file, the Guideline agent
  checks the semantics of the input/out parameters, and sends a translation
  request to the Ontology Agent to translate the input messages from the HL7
  RIM to the message schema specified in the OWL-S file. The same procedure
  is repeated when the output is received from the Web service.
- The "Get Data Actions" can be used to represent either references to EHR
  document or to vital signs of the patient to be retrieved from wireless medical
  sensor devices through Sensor Web services. The Sensor Web services are also
  invoked as the Medical Web service, by contacting with the Ontology Agent
  to mediate the input and output parameters.

    Whenever a reference to a clinical information presented in an EHR doc-
  ument is encountered by the Guideline Agent in the guideline definition, the
  Guideline Agent sends a request to the EHR agent, with the document identifiers previously filled by the Agent Factory Agent, and also with the semantic
  annotation of the clinical data to be extracted from the EHR document. As
  presented, the EHR agent parses the document, consults to Ontology agent
  when necessary to reconciliate the coded terms one another, and as a response sends the requested content in HL7 RIM to the Guideline Agent. The
  Guideline Agent stores all of these clinical data, sensor data to a global variable pool, so that other handlers such as "Decision Step Handler" can make
  use of them when necessary.

- The "Message Actions" are used to generate alarm messages within the clinical guideline execution. When the Guideline Agent encounters a "Message Action" during clinical guideline execution; it immediately constructs an alarm message by combining information coming through guideline definition and agent properties. Alarm message, healthcare role id to whom the message is to be delivered and alarm urgency parameters are retrieved from guideline definition whereas patient and guideline ids are retrieved from agent properties. The constructed alarm messages are transmitted to "Alarm Distribution Agent", which actuates the delivery. The transmission is performed through JADE [24] messaging and ontology facilities.

3.5. Alarm Distribution Agent

Alarm Distribution Agent is responsible from accurate and punctual delivery of alarm messages to the healthcare users. It triggers the distribution of the alarms when it receives such a request from the Guideline Agent.

Alarm Distribution Agent employs a role based delivery mechanism, in which the real responsible healthcare users for a patient-guideline pair are determined based to the role id indicated by the alarm message. There are four pre-determined role ids which are administrator, doctor, nurse and patient relative. Through a web based interface, the healthcare users can subscribe to receive alarm messages related with a specific patient guideline pair. Alarm messages are delivered to the users through three different mediums: SMS, GoogleTalk Instant Messaging and secure e-mail. The users can customize their preferences for receiving alarm messages in different urgencies (medium type, number of deliveries, acknowledgement requirement, routing option etc.) through a web based user interface. User preferences are stored as JESS [33] rules. These rules are executed in delivery time and the delivery terms are determined.

Acknowledgement facility is a confirmation mechanism in order to ensure reliable delivery of the alarm messages. With this option, users are required to confirm that they have received the alarm messages. For e-mail and Instant Messaging, the acknowledgment method is simply replying to the message; SMS acknowledgment is realized through delivery confirmation message. In case that the message is not acknowledged, it is re-sent to the user for a number of times determined based on user preferences; if the message is still unacknowledged; it is routed to another healthcare user which is specified by the healthcare user.

3.6. Monitoring Agent

Monitoring Agent presents a graphical user interface to the healthcare users for clinical guidelines. Through the Monitoring Agent Interface, healthcare users can start/stop and monitor the execution of clinical guidelines by interacting with the guideline agent. In addition to these, guideline agent can consult to the healthcare professionals' decisions through this component.

Guideline execution is monitored on a user friendly interface which is composed of three parts. The main part of the interface depicts the flowchart of the clinical guideline model, whereas the others are for the message sequence and legend of the flowchart. Guideline execution can be traced on the flowchart model. The status of the guideline steps (committed/ongoing/ not visited) are identified with different colors. User can click on the steps to get detailed information about the step. In the detailed information screen, user can view the tasks, retrieved patient data (sensor, EHR etc.) and the invoked medical services within these tasks. In case that, the medical experts decision is needed, Monitoring Agent displays a pop-up window for consulting. In this way, input is provided for Guideline Agent. The communication between Monitoring Agent and Guideline Agent is realized via JADE[24] messages. The messages are implemented in JADE ontologies in order to structure a well defined message format for monitoring and consulting. The communication between agents is based on a publish-subscribe mechanism in which multiple monitoring agents can be subscribed to one single Guideline Agent.

Apart from these, an important outcome of the Monitoring Agent is the visual model that it provides for clinical guidelines. This visual flow-chart model can be utilized as an educative medium in training healthcare professionals.

4. Conclusion

The architecture described in this paper is realized within the scope of IST-27074 SAPHIRE project. The prototype implementation is achieved using JADE Agent Platform.

The SAPHIRE has two pilot applications: in the hospital pilot we address the bedside monitoring of subacute phase of the patients suffering from myocardial infarction; in the homecare scenario we address the homecare monitoring of the rehabilitation of the cardiovascular patients undergone a revascularization therapy. A more detailed discussion of SAPHIRE pilot applications can be found in [34]. Through these pilot applications, the system aims to increase adherence to the guidelines, hence provide standardization to care processes, to reduce costs of care with optimal benefit for the patient and doctor, to reduce human error in hospital events/complications and finally to provide a feedback system for medical staff in training.

References

[1] "Demographic change & ageing: The possible role of ICT, Lutz Kubitscke," http://ec.europa.eu/information_society/events/phs_2007/docs/slides/phs2007-kubitschke-s2b.pdf.

[2] M. Field and K. Lohr, *Guidelines for Clinical Practice: From development to use.* Washington DC: Institute of Medicine, National Academy Press, 1992.

[3] "Guideline Interchange Format (GLIF) 3," InterMed Collaboratory, Tech. Rep., 2004.

[4] A. Seyfang, S. Miksch, and M. Marcos, " Combining Diagnosis and Treatment using Asbru," *International Journal of Medical Informatics*, vol. 68 (1-3), pp. 49–57, 2002.

[5] M. Peleg, O. Ogunyemi, and S. Tu, "Using features of Arden Syntax with object-oriented medical data models for guideline modeling," in *Proceedings of AMIA Symposium*, 2001, pp. 523–527.

[6] S. Tu and M. Musen, "Modeling Data and Knowledge in the EON Guideline Architecture," in *Proceedings of MedInfo 2001*, London, UK, 2001, pp. 280–284.

[7] D. Wang, M. Peleg, S. Tu, A. Boxwala, O. Ogunyemi, Q. Zeng, A. Greenes, V. Patel, and E. Shortliffe, "Design and Implementation of GLIF3 guideline execution engine," *Journal of Biomedical Informatics,*, vol. 37, pp. 305–318, 2004.

[8] P. Terenziani, G. Molino, and M. Torchio, "A modular approach for representing and executing clinical guidelines," *Artificial Intelligence in Medicine,*, vol. 23(3), pp. 249–276, 2001.

[9] Y. Shahar, O. Young, E. Shalom, M. Galperin, A. Mayaffit, R. Moskovitch, and A. Hessing, " A Framework for a Distributed, Hybrid, Multiple-Ontology Clinical-Guideline Library and Automated Guideline-Support Tools," *Journal of Biomedical Informatics,*, vol. 37, no. 5, pp. 325–344, 2004.

[10] M. F. et al., "Medical decision support systems: Old dilemmas and new paradigms?" *Methods Inf Med.,*, vol. 42(3), pp. 190–198, 2003.

[11] M. Entwiste and R. Shiffman, "Turning Guidelines into Practice: Making It Happen With Standards - Part 1," *Healthcare and Informatics Review Online, March 2005*, 2005.

[12] "Open ECG Portal," http://www.openecg.net/.

[13] "HL7 XML Standards and FDA," http://www.fda.gov/cder/regulatory/ersr/2003_06_17_XML/index.htm.

[14] "IMED - International Medical Equipment Developing Co. Ltd." http://www.imed.hu/index2.php.

[15] "ecgML," http://ijsr32.infj.ulst.ac.uk/~e10110731/ecgML/.

[16] "ISO/IEEE 11073-10101:2004:Health informatics, Point-of-care medical device communication, Part 10101: Nomenclature," http://www.iso.org/iso/en/ CatalogueDetailPage.CatalogueDetail?CSNUMBER=37890.

[17] "XDS - Cross-Enterprise Document Sharing," http://hcxw2k1.nist.gov/wiki /index.php/XDS_-_Cross-Enterprise_Document_Sharing.

[18] HL7 Clinical Document Architecture, Release 2.0. http://hl7.org/library /Committees/structure/CDA.ReleaseTwo.CommitteeBallot03.Aug.2004.zip.

[19] HL7ReferenceInformationModel. http://www.hl7.org/v3ballot8/html/foundationdocuments/welcome/index.htm.

[20] "Logical Observation Identifiers Names and Codes (LOINC)," http://www.regenstrief.org/loinc/.

[21] "SNOMED Clinical Terms," http://www.snomed.org/.

[22] WHO, "International Statistical Classification of Diseases and Related Health Problems, 10th Revision (ICD-10), Second Edition," World Health Organization, Geneva, Switzerland, Tech. Rep., 2005, http://www.who.int/whosis/icd10/.

[23] "Nationaal ICT Instituut in de Zorg," http://www.nictiz.nl.

[24] "JAVA Agent Development Platform, JADE," http://jade.tilab.com/.

[25] "Spine- NHS Connecting for Health,"
http://www.connectingforhealth.nhs.uk/systems
andservices/spine.

[26] "Canada Health Infoway," http://www.infoway-inforoute.ca/en/home/home.aspx.

[27] "FIPA Ontology Service Specification,"
http://www.tipa.org/specs/fipa00086/XC00086C.html.

[28] A. Dogac, G. Laleci, S. Kirbas, Y. Kabak, S. Sinir, A. Yildiz, and Y. Gurcan,
"Artemis: Deploying Semantically Enriched Web Services in the Healthcare Domain," *Information Systems Journal, special issue on Semantic Web and Web Services*, vol. 31(4-5), pp. 321–339, 2006.

[29] V. Bicer, G. Laleci, A. Dogac, and Y. Kabak, "Artemis Message Exchange Framework: Semantic Interoperability of Exchanged Messages in the Healthcare Domain,"
ACM Sigmod Record, vol. 34, no. 3, September 2005.

[30] "Unified Medical Language System (UMLS),"
http://www.nlm.nih.gov/research/umls/.

[31] "SAPHIRE Project Deliverable 5.2.1: Clinical Guideline models to be used in Clinical
Decision Processes ," http://www.srdc.metu.edu.tr/webpage/projects/saphire
/deliverables/SAPHIRED5.2.1Final.doc.

[32] G. Laleci and A. Dogac, "SAPHIRE: A Multi-agent System for Deploying Semantically Enriched Clinical Guidelines in Heterogeneous Healthcare Environments,"
Submitted to Elsevier Information Systems Journal.

[33] "Jess, the Rule Engine for the Java Platform," http://herzberg.ca.sandia.gov/jess/.

[34] O. Nee, A. Hein, T. Gorath, N. H. G. B. Laleci, M. Yuksel, M. Olduz, I. Tasyurt,
U. Orhan, A. Dogac, A. Fruntelata, S. Ghiorghe, and R.Ludwig, "SAPHIRE: Intelligent Healthcare Monitoring based on Semantic Interoperability Platform - Pilot Applications," *Accepted forIEEE Proceedings Communications-Special Issue on
Telemedicine and a-Health Communication Systems*.

Gokce B. Laleci, Asuman Dogac, Mehmet Olduz, Ibrahim Tasyurt, Mustafa Yuksel and
Alper Okcan
Middle East Technical University
Computer Engineering Department, SRDC
Inonu Bulvari
06531 Ankara / TURKEY
e-mail: asuman@srdc.metu.edu.tr

Whitestein Series in Software Agent Technologies, 45–63
© 2007 Birkhäuser Verlag Basel/Switzerland

EU PROVENANCE Project:
An Open Provenance Architecture for
Distributed Applications

Javier Vázquez-Salceda, Sergio Álvarez, Tamás Kifor, László Z. Varga,
Simon Miles, Luc Moreau and Steven Willmott

Abstract. The concept of *provenance* is already well understood in the study of fine
art where it refers to the trusted, documented history of some work of art. Given that
documented history, the object attains an authority that allows scholars to understand
and appreciate its importance and context relative to other works of art. This same
concept of provenance may also be applied to data and information generated within
a computer system; particularly when the information is subject to regulatory control
over an extended period of time. Today's distributed architectures (not only Agent technologies, but also Web Services' and GRID architectures) suffer from limitations, such
as lack of mechanisms to trace results. Provenance enables users to trace how a particular result has been arrived at by identifying the individual and aggregated services
that produced a particular output. In this chapter we present the main results of the EU
PROVENANCE project and how these can be valuable in agent-mediated healthcare
applications. For the latter we describe the Organ Transplant Management Application
(OTMA), one of the demonstrator applications developed.

Keywords. Provenance, software agents, healthcare.

1. Introduction

The importance of understanding the process by which a result was generated is fundamental to many real-life applications in science, engineering, medical domain, supply
management, etc. Without such information, users cannot reproduce, analyze or validate
processes or experiments. Provenance is therefore important to enable users, scientists
and engineers to trace how a particular result came about.

Most distributed solutions can be seen as networks of computational services at distributed locations, which operate by dynamically creating services at opportunistic moments to satisfy the need of some user. These services may belong to different stakeholders operating under various different policies about information sharing. The results provided by such a composition of services must, however, be trusted by the user and yet, when the services disband, the following question arises: how are we to obtain the verification of the processes that contributed to the final result?

This problem is especially relevant for distributed medical applications. In such applications the data (containing the healthcare history of a single patient), the workflow (of the procedures carried out on that patient) and the logs (recording meaningful events in those procedures) are distributed among several heterogeneous and autonomous information systems. Communication and coordination between organizations and among members of a medical team are critical issues the distributed application should address, in order to ease information sharing and to provide some support to distributed decision making. One approach to model and implement distributed medical applications is the use of agent-based techniques [10]. Modelling application components as agents with some degree of autonomy eases the development phase as it makes it easier to reflect the decentralized nature of the network of healthcare institutions and actors involved in a healthcare process, and also eases the integration of systems owned and developed by different authorities and also humans in the system, by encapsulating them in agents or agent-mediating interfaces.

Even when using agent technologies, the distributed nature of healthcare institutions sometimes makes it really hard to obtain overall views of the treatments of patients, because documentation of the healthcare history and therapy of a patient is split into independent healthcare institutions. However, more and more healthcare applications tend to move towards a user-centric perspective. In order to provide better, user-centered healthcare services, the treatment of a patient requires viewing the processes and data as a whole. Although agent-based cooperation techniques and standardized electronic healthcare record exchange techniques support the semantic interoperation between healthcare providers, we still face the problem of the reunification of the different pieces of the therapy of a single patient executed at different places. Currently there are some countries that have no unification method for patient healthcare records; each region in the country or even each institution inside a region may have its own medical record system, sometimes not even fully electronic, and with no automatic healthcare record exchange mechanisms. Therefore, it is not uncommon for doctors to depend on the patients themselves in order to include data from previous treatments and tests. Furthermore, in medical (and other critical application) domains, there is also a need to provide ways to analyze the performance of distributed healthcare services, and to be able to carry out audits of the system to assess that, for a given patient, the proper decisions were made and the proper procedures were followed.

In this chapter we present a new approach to both capture the distributed medical treatment of a patient in different health institutions in an integrated, patient oriented way, and to register all meaningful events related to a patient's treatment for further analysis, not only for audit purposes but also for medical staff to detect problems in the medical

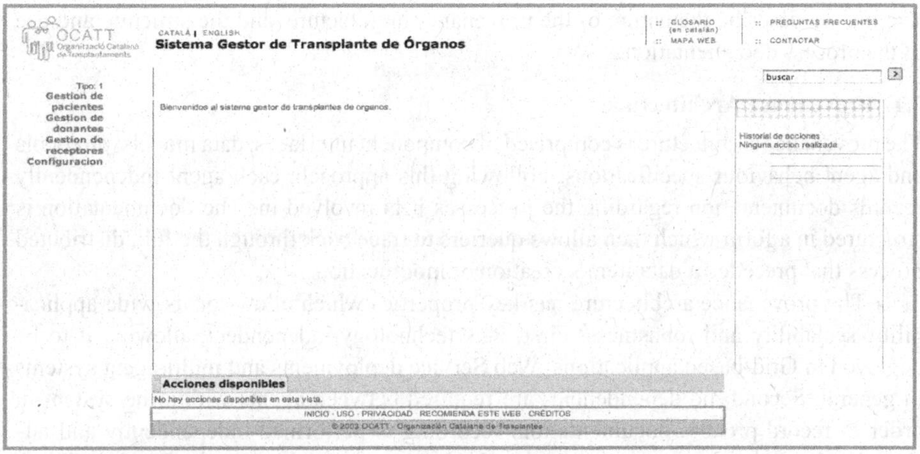

FIGURE 1. The Organ Transplant Management Application (OTMA) user interface

processes (e.g., bottlenecks or lack of timely information) in the processes they are involved into. Our main hypothesis is that trust in results produced by an agent-mediated distributed healthcare system can be increased if the provenance of each of the particular results can be known (e.g., where the patient was treated, who has been involved in each medical treatment, who has taken decisions and which were the basis for such decisions).

The content is structured as follows: in Section 2 we define the *provenance* concept and describe the the technological developments in the EU PROVENANCE Project; then in Section 3 we briefly present the Organ Transplant Management Application (OTMA), which we will use as example of the use of provenance in agent-mediated healthcare applications; in Section 4 we describe the process undertaken to make the OTMA application *provenance-aware*; in Section 5 we explain how the recorded provenance data can be used to analyse relevant events related to a medical process; in Section 6 we describe the problem on connecting medical process documentation between heathcare institutions; in Section 7 we discuss the privacy issues that may arise by introducing provenance recording in healthcare applications; finally in Section 8 we conclude by summarizing our approach and referring to related work in the literature.

2. Provenance

A key contribution of the IST-funded EU PROVENANCE project, and a technology which underpins the rest of the work described in this chapter, was the development of a *provenance architecture* [6]. Where an application is integrated with an implementation of the architecture, users have facilities to determine the *provenance* of data items produced by that application, i.e., the causes of a data item being as it is. The provenance of an item is extracted from the documentation of processes occurring within the application. In this section, we describe the nature of the provenance architecture, and the structure and use of the process documentation.

2.1. Provenance Architecture

The provenance architecture is comprised of component interfaces, data models, protocols and agent behaviour specifications. Following this approach, each agent independently records documentation regarding the processes it is involved in. The documentation is structured in a form which then allows queriers to trace back through the full, distributed process that preceded a data item's creation or modification.

The provenance architecture has key properties which allow for its wide applicability, scalability and robustness. First, it is technology-independent, allowing it to be deployed in Grid-based applications, Web Service deployments and multi-agent systems in general. Second, no dependencies are required between agents within the system in order to record process documentation: recording is performed independently and autonomously, and no agent is assumed to have access to the state of any other. Third, while conceptually being recorded during execution, documentation of a process can be recorded asynchronously from the process itself. Both the latter two issues are important factors in preserving the performance of large-scale systems. Finally, the application will not be adversely affected if accurate documentation is not available, because few assumptions are made about the documentation. For example, documentation can be complete or partial (for instance, when the computation has not terminated yet); it can be accurate or inaccurate; it can present conflicting or consensual views by the agents involved; it can describe the process at differing levels of detail and abstraction.

Aside from the architecture itself, the project produced an open source reference implementation [1] and a methodology that aids application developers in integrating and exploiting the provenance architecture in their systems [9]. The research was applied not only to healthcare, but also distributed aerospace simulations and bioinformatics experiments, and potential uses were explored in many other sciences [8].

2.2. Process Documentation

The provenance of a data item is represented in a computer system by a set of *p-assertions* made by the actors involved in the process that created it. A p-assertion is a specific piece of information documenting some step of the process made by an actor and pertains to the process. We follow a simple model of process, whereby agents communicate information via *messages*, the sending of one message by one agent and the receiving of that same message by another agent being called an *interaction*. A process consists of a series of exchanges of messages between agents, and processing of the data within those messages by the agents. There are three kinds of p-assertions that capture an explicit description of the flow of data in a process:

- An *interaction p-assertion* is an assertion of the contents of a message by an agent that has sent or received that message.
- A *relationship p-assertion* is an assertion about an interaction, made by an agent that describes how the actor obtained data sent in that interaction by applying some function to input received in other interactions.

- An *actor state p-assertion* is an assertion made by an agent about its internal state in the context of a specific interaction.

Within the architecture, a long-term facility for storing the process documentation described above is defined, called a *provenance store*. A provenance store is used to manage and provide controlled access to the representation of the provenance of a specific data element. As part of the architecture, a recording and two querying interfaces are defined for the provenance store. The *process documentation query* interface allows p-assertions to be retrieved singly or in groups by criteria. The *provenance query* interface returns a trace of all process documentation in the process producing a given data item, i.e., that item's provenance. It allows the results of the query to be scoped to that relevant to the querier, e.g., within a given period of time or at a given level of abstraction.

In the case of agent-mediated healthcare systems, by recording documentation on all the medical processes related to a given patient, one can then re-construct the treatment history of the patient. Therefore, making an agent-mediated healthcare system *provenance-aware* provides a way to have a unified view of a patient's medical record along with its provenance, i.e., to connect each part of the medical record with the processes in the real world producing it and/or the individuals, teams or units responsible for each piece of data within it.

3. OTM/EHCR: applying provenance in agent-mediated healthcare applications

In this chapter we demonstrate the potential usage of provenance in distributed healthcare systems by describing our experience in the domain of Organ Transplant Management. Distributed Organ Transplant Management is an excellent case study of both provenance and the privacy issues of provenance. Treatment of patients through the transplantation of organs or tissue is one of the most complex distributed medical processes currently carried out. This complexity arises not only from the difficulty of the surgery itself but also from the fact that it is a distributed problem involving several locations (donating hospital, potential recipient hospitals, test laboratories and organ transplant authorities), a wide range of associated processes, rules and decision making. Depending on the country where a transplant is being carried out, procedures and the level of electronic automation of information / decision making may vary significantly. However, it is recognized worldwide that ICT solutions which increase the speed and accuracy of decision making could have a very significant positive impact on patient care outcomes. In [12, 13] we presented CARREL, an Agent-Mediated Electronic Institution for the distribution of organs and tissues for transplantation purposes. One of the aims of the CARREL system was to help speeding up the allocation process of solid organs for transplantation to improve graft survival rates. Several prototypes of the CARREL system have been developed using JADE [3]. Although medical practitioners positively evaluated the prototypes, system administrators proved to be very reluctant to manage agent platforms for critical medical applications, and prototypes didn't go through. In [14] a connection between Agent Communication Languages and Web Service Inter-Communication was proposed. This

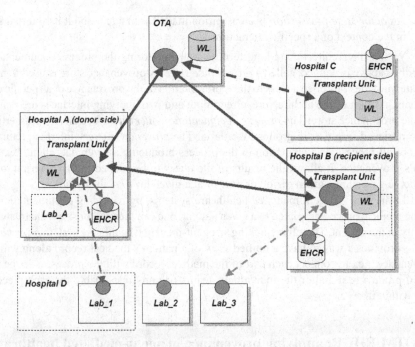

FIGURE 2.   Actors in the OTMA system. Actors communicate and coordinate with each other through agents (circles in figure).

connection allows us to implement agent systems by means of web services which can
interact following the same FIPA protocols [5]. With this approach we developed a new
prototype, the Organ Transplant Management Application (OTMA) which uses standard
web service technology and it is able to interact with the provenance stores in order to
keep track of the distributed execution of the allocation process for audit purposes.

Management of the electronic health records distributed in different institutions
is provided by the Electronic Healthcare Record System (EHCR). Its internal architecture provides the structures to build a part of or the entire patient's healthcare record
drawn from any number of heterogeneous databases systems in order to exchange it with
other healthcare information systems. The EHCR architecture has two external interfaces:
1) a Web Service that receives and sends messages (following FIPA protocols [5] and the
ENV13606 pre-standard format [4] for the content) for remote medical applications, and
2) a Java API for local medical applications that can be used to access the EHCR store
directly.

Figure 2 summarizes the different administrative domains (solid boxes) and units
(dashed boxes) that are modeled in the OTMA system. Each of these interact with each
other through agents (circles in the figure) that exchange information and requests through
messages. In a transplant management scenario, one or more hospital units may be involved: the hospital transplant unit, one or several units that provide laboratory tests

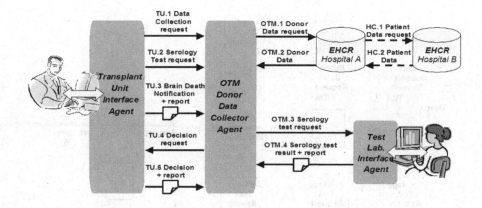

FIGURE 3.   Example of interaction in the OTMA system.

and the Electronic Healthcare Record (EHCR) subsystem which manages the healthcare records for each institution. The diagram also shows some of the data stores that are involved: apart from the patient records, these include stores for the transplant units and the Organ Transplant Authority (OTA) recipient waiting lists (WL). Hospitals that are the origin of a donation also keep records of the donations performed, while hospitals that are recipients of the donation may include such information in the recipient's patient record. The OTA has also its own records of each donation, stored case by case.

4. Making the OTMA system provenance-aware

Making the OTMA system provenance-aware presented three challenging issues: a) the provenance of most of the data is not the execution of computational services, but decisions and actions carried out by real people in the real world (this is discussed in this section); b) past treatments of a given patient in other institutions may be relevant to the current decisions in the current institution, so information of the processes undertaken in those previous treatments should be connected to the provenance information of a current process (this is discussed in Section 6); c) the agent with provenance information knows much more about the patient than any other agent in the system, so there are privacy risks to be mitigated (this is discussed in Section 7).

In the case of the OTMA system, each organizational unit is represented by an agent-mediated service. Staff members of each unit can connect to the unit services by means of graphical user interfaces (e.g., see the one in Figure 1). The distributed execution of the OTM services is modeled as the interaction between the agents, and recorded as interaction p-assertions and relationship p-assertions. As in the OTM scenario a decision depends on the human making the decision, additional actor state p-assertions are recorded, containing further information on why the particular decision was made and, if available, the identities(s) of the team members involved in the decision.

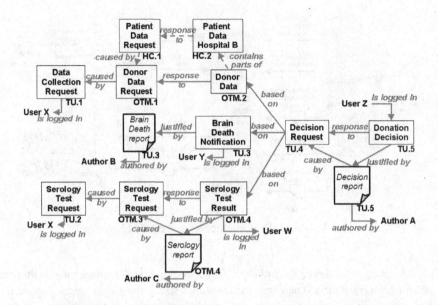

FIGURE 4. Example of provenance trace for the Donation Decision.

To illustrate how provenance is handled in the OTMA system, let us see how the provenance of a medical decision is recorded. Figure 3 shows a simplified view over a subset of the donation process. In this example a patient (who has previously given consent to donate his organs) enters into a given hospital in critical condition. As the patient's health declines and in foresight of a potential organ donation, one of the doctors requests the full health record for the patient and then orders a serology test [1] through the OTMA system. After the patient enters into a severe comma, a doctor declares a "brain death" condition for this patient and such relevant event is logged in the system (along with the report certifying the brain death). When the system detects that all requested data and analysis results have been obtained, the system sends a request to a doctor to make a decision about the patient being a potential donor. This decision is explained in a report that is submitted as the decision's justification and which is logged in the system.

Figure 3 shows the OTMA agents for this small scenario and their interactions. The Transplant Unit User Interface Agent passes requests (TU.1, TU.2) to the OTM Donor Data Collector Agent, which then gets the electronic record from the EHCR system (OTM.1, OTM.2). Sometimes all or parts of the record are not in the same institution but located in another institution (HC.1, HC.2). The Donor Data Collector Agent also sends the request for a serology test to the laboratory and gets back the result (OTM.4), along with a detailed report of the test. Reports are also passed in the case of the Brain Death notification (TU.3) and the final decision report (TU.5).

---

[1] A serology test is usually performed over blood samples to detect viruses (HIV, Hepatitis B/C, syphilis, herpes or Epstein-Barr virus), which, if present in the organ, can pass to the recipient.

Figure 4 graphically represents the subset of the p-assertions produced by the provenance-aware OTMA which are related to the mini-scenario described in Figure 3. The part of the process that happens within the electronic system is represented by interaction p-assertions (regular boxes) for all interactions (TU.x, OTM.x, HC.x), and relationship p-assertions (`response_to`, `caused_by`, `based_on`) capturing dependencies between data. Even though what happens in the system parallels what happens in the real world, as we already said this is not enough to fully determine the provenance of a given decision. To solve this, we connect the electronic process to the real world by adding actor state p-assertions stating who logged the information in the system (`is_logged_in`) and when (not shown in picture), which are the reports that justify a given state in the system (`justified_by`), who are the authors of these reports (`authored_by`) and when the action reported was performed or the decision taken (not shown).

5. Analyzing the distributed medical process through provenance

Storing provenance documentation instead of the, more common, standard log systems, has the advantage that the provenance representation is stored in a way that complex queries can be performed over it, which allows a provenance-aware system to extract valuable information to validate some of the steps taken into a (medical) process, or even to make an audit of the system over a period of time.

In the OTMA system, apart from periodical audits, transplant coordinators also want to ask the following types of provenance questions, related to a given patient (donor or recipient) or to the fate of a given organ:

- Where did the medical information used on each step of the process come from?
- When was a decision taken, and what was the basis of the decision?
- Which medical actors were asked to provide medical data for a decision?
- Which medical actor refused to provide medical data for a decision?
- Which medical actor was the source of some piece of information?
- What kind of medical record was available to actors at each step of the process?
- When was a given medical process carried out, and who was responsible for it?

All these kind of questions can be answered by querying the provenance store. A query will give as a result (a subset of) the provenance representation graph of the process related to the query. If we use as an example the graph in Figure 4, by following the edges from the "Donation Decision" p-assertion we can trace the provenance of the donation decision, how it was based in some data and test requests, how a brain death notification is also involved, who requested the information, where it came from (in some cases it might come from the EHCR of another hospital), and who authored the justifying reports in the main steps of the process.

In those cases (as in Figure 4) where the decision might be based on medical data coming from tests and medical treatments carried out in other institutions, another issue to solve is the following: how to find, retrieve and incorporate the provenance of the data coming from the other institution? If these institutions have also provenance-aware systems and the provenance stores of the different institutions are connected, to solve the aforementioned problem is to solve the issue of matching the different p-assertions related to the same patient. If this match is done, then actors can make p-assertions that link together the separate sets of p-assertions to create a larger provenance document providing an integrated view of the healthcare history of the patient. The result (not shown on Figure 4) would be that the p-assertions related to Patient Data Hospital B would be linked to the set of p-assertions already part of the provenance of the Donation Decision (by means of the method that we will describe in Section 6).

Collectively the p-assertions can be seen as describing a distributed process, spanning space as well as time. Every relationship described is causal, i.e., between the cause of something happening and the effect of it happening, and is therefore also temporal, i.e., causes always come before effects. Furthermore, extra information can be added to provide further detail. For example, an actor may record, as an actor state p-assertion, the time shown on their local clock. Together, the structured documentation of processes allows a rich set of questions to be asked about what occurred, why, when and by whom and, in the OTMA system, such a process may be a patient's healthcare history

6. Connecting medical process documentation to create a patient's integrated view

As seen in the previous section, in order to be able to create an integrated view of a patient's healthcare history, there must be a series of links between any two p-assertions of the process documentation created by each healthcare institution. The links in the process documentation are interaction p-assertions and relationship p-assertions which connect together the p-assertions of agents in the process. In usual service-oriented applications these links are created by use of a common identifier, called an interaction key, for both parties, sender and receiver, in an interaction. If two agents record p-assertions using the same interaction key, we can determine that their actions are part of the same process, and therefore both are part of the provenance of the process' output. We can record p-assertions with the same interaction key, if the two agents exchange that key, which means they must electronically interact.

In typical business or e-science applications, the agents participating in the process are in contact with each other and exchange documented messages while there is an interaction between them. In this case we say that there is *direct interaction* between the agents. However medical processes, and some other types of processes, are different, because the physicians treating the same patient may not be in direct contact. A typical example would be the following: a patient P is treated by one physician in health institution $H1$; then patient P is released from $H1$; months later the patient goes to another physician in health institution $H2$ with symptoms of another disease. Sometimes there may even be a medical relationship between the two treatments, for example because the second disease is a consequence of the first disease, but neither the patient nor the physicians are aware of this. In this case, the physicians are not in contact with the each other. ¿From the process documentation point of view it is also important to note that the physicians do not know each other's identity, and they may use different identifiers to identify

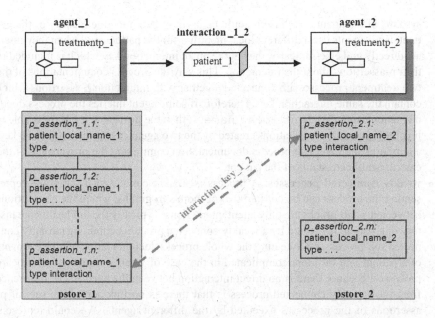

FIGURE 5.   Process documentation in strongly connected processes.

the patient in their process documentations, because the identities cannot be revealed for privacy reasons. This way the p-assertions belonging to the same patient cannot be linked together automatically, because the p-assertions cannot be located by the patient identifier. In this case we say that there is *latent interaction* between the physician agents. Note that the patient usually cannot determine the link between the current treatment and the previous one. This is not only because the patient does not remember the previous treatment, but also because the second physician cannot locate the p-assertions made by the first physician, due to lack of known identifiers.

Based on the distinction between direct and indirect electronic interactions we can define two types of processes: *strongly connected processes* and *weakly connected processes*. The processes can be seen as graphs, where the nodes represent the activities executed by the agents alone and the arcs represent the interactions between the agents. The interactions are either latent or direct.

- **strongly connected processes**: A process is strongly connected if the graph representing the process contains only direct interactions. Figure 5 shows the model of a strongly connected process and its process documentation. Agents 1 and 2 represent the physicians who are the actors of treatment processes 1 (treatmentp_1) and 2 (treatmentp_2). When agent 1 sends the patient to agent 2 in a documented way, the p-assertions about this interaction are recorded by agents 1 and 2. In a medical application we cannot use the globally unique identifier of the patient in the local systems of the agents, because it could be used to determine the identity of the patient. Both agents use a different local identifier for the patient, and when they interact directly and electronically, they agree on an interaction key which is included in their p-assertions about the interaction. This way the process documentations of the two treatment processes are connected together with interaction p-assertions which contain the same interaction key. Therefore if some agent queries the process documentation using `patient_local_name_1`, then the provenance system is able to link the process documentations created by the two agents using the interaction key, and returns the complete process documentation comprising the provenance of the current healthcare status of the patient.

- **weakly connected processes**: A process is weakly connected if the graph representing the process can be cut into two or more sub-graphs, where the connections between the sub-graphs are only latent interactions. Typically the full healthcare history of a patient is created by a weakly connected process containing strongly connected sub-processes. Collecting the whole process documentation of all treatments of a patient is a bit more complicated in the case of weakly connected healthcare processes, because there is no direct interaction between the agents. The difference from the strongly connected process is that there is no link across the sets of p-assertions of the processes executed by the different agents. We could represent this situation graphically if, in Figure 5 above, we delete both the direct interaction (`interaction_1_2`) and the link between the medical processes documentation (`interaction_key_1_2`). If we want to retrieve the complete provenance of the current healthcare status of the patient, then we would like to retrieve both sets. In addition to this, the agents are unable to connect the two sets of p-assertions, because even if agent 2 finds out somehow that treatment process 2 is some way a consequence of treatment process 1, it does not know the local identifier of the patient used by the other agent and cannot locate the relevant p-assertions made by agent 1. Note that although the patient usually presents to the physicians its global identifier (such as its social security number), this global identifier cannot be used in process documentation for privacy reasons, as discussed later in Section 7.

The basic transplant process of OTMA is strongly connected, because there are always direct interactions between the actors. However when they retrieve the full EHCR of the patient, which may contain data from previous treatments, the transplant process becomes "infected" with the latent interactions of the EHCR creation process.

In order to provide a solution to the problem of process documentation creation resulting from the lack of direct interaction between the agents, we need to find an intermediate way of interaction. This can be done with the help of an institution in a higher hierarchical level, which is in contact with both agents and knows about the patient as well. Medical domains are usually regulated by national and international bodies which assure that there are services which give a global identifier to the patient, such as the national security number. As we said before, the global identifier should not be used in documentation of privacy-aware medical processes, because regulations ordain the separation of medical information and personal identification. The fact that these data cannot be stored

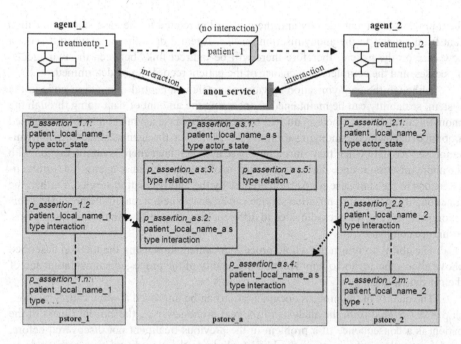

FIGURE 6.   Connecting process documentation in weakly connected processes.

together leads to the use of anonymised identifiers to connect medical and personal data. Because of this, agent-mediated healthcare systems usually contain an anonymisation service to convert real patient identifiers to anonymised patient identifiers.

Figure 6 shows how the method of creating intermediate interactions and intermediate links in the process documentation works. In the first step of this method, we locate already existing anonymisation service in the application. If there is no such service, then we introduce it into the application. The service is called anon_service in the figure.

The second important element of the method is that the anonymisation service makes p-assertions about its own processing. Whenever the anonymisation service is asked to create a new patient identifier, then the anonymisation service puts an actor state p-assertion into the provenance store about the creation of the patient identity. This p-assertion does not contain the global patient identifier, only the anonymised identifier.

The third important element of the method is that each time a new case of a patient is started, the agents notify the anonymisation service. This notification is a direct interaction, therefore it is documented in the process documentation. This is shown in Figure . When agent 1 starts a new case on the patient, it makes an actor state p-assertion about the start of the case and notifies the anonymisation service that the case started. The direct interaction of the notification is recorded in the provenance store with interaction p-assertions on both sides. The anonymisation service knows the identity of the patient, and asserts a relationship p-assertion between the p-assertion related to the creation of the anonymised patient identity and the p-assertion related to the case start notification sent from agent 1 to the anonymisation service. Agent 2 does the same when it starts a new case on the patient, therefore there will be indirect links between the two agents' processes, and the complete provenance of the patient record can be determined.

Although the anonymisation service is somehow a central interaction node in the system, scalability can be maintained. Concerning the amount of data going through the anonymisation service, there is no real bottleneck, because agents communicate limited amount of data with the anonymisation service. Moreover, the agents contact the anonymisation service only when they start a new case and then later there is no interaction with the anonymisation service during the execution of the case, because agents link further p-assertions to the start case p-assertion created by the anonymisation service. Further, the functionality of the anonymisation service can be distributed in real implemented systems among cooperating services allocated to different hierarchy levels, like countries, regions, insurance companies, etc.

The ability to return the whole process documentation using the method described above allows the agents to improve both the quality of the process documentation and of their own activities.

The quality of the process documentation can be improved if some causal relationship is discovered from the analysis of the real processes, e.g., the current illness of the patient is a consequence of a problem in the previous treatment not discovered before. In this case, the agents can insert additional links to the already existing process documentation created together with the help of the anonymisation service. The additionally inserted links document the real world causal relationships between the p-assertions of the already existing process documentation. Because the links created with the help of the anonymisation service integrate the p-assertions relevant to a single patient into a single graph, any p-assertion in this graph can be located and identified, so the link related to the real world causal relationship can be added.

The agents can improve the quality of their own activities with the help of the integrated process documentation. Now that the process documentation is integrated, agent 2 can retrieve the p-assertions of agent 1 and use this information in the current treatment.

7. Protection of Privacy in Provenance-aware Application

The issue of privacy in healthcare applications is extremely important. As reflected in the famous Hippocratic oath, protection of individuals' health-related data has been a continued concern of the medical body from the very beginning of the medical practice. There exist considerable efforts to put into practice a body of policies which ensure the protection of medical data in a scenario of massive use of computers in the health sector. Regulations define guidelines about the adequate organizational and technical measures that must be taken in medical information systems. The most important of these guidelines concerns the separation of data: as a general rule, the design of data structures, procedures and access control policies must be such that they allow the separation of a) identifiers and data related to a person's identity, b) administrative data, c) medical data, and d) genetic data. Such separation must ensure that no unauthorized person can connect the identity of the patient with his medical or genetic data.

In EHCR systems, and in the OTMA system discussed above, a typical solution for the separation of identity information and medical data is the anonymised identifier. The anonymised identifier is generated from a real patient identifier, and medical data is stored together with this anonymised identifier. If we know the real patient identifier, then we can find the corresponding medical data, but from the medical data we cannot find out the identity of the patient.

An anonymisation method must keep identifiers in secret during remote database management. The database is updated frequently, items are added and removed so we implemented the function on the client side of the database, i.e., in the web application, in order to keep the identifiers unknown for unauthorized people and applications. The function has the following features:

- It generates an unsigned long output for every unsigned long input.
- It uses two parameters to make the algorithm safer and reusable.
- It is deterministic, i.e., the output is always the same for a specific input value.
- It is injective i.e., it generates different output values for different inputs.
- The source code is private. That means that the only person who knows is the developer of the code.
- The final binary is deployed to a properly obfuscated JAR file to make the code breaking harder.

The above methods protect privacy in non provenance-aware healthcare applications, however when we make agent systems provenance-aware, we introduce the provenance store into the system, which needs additional protection, because there is a conflict between provenance and privacy. While for provenance we need as much information as possible about the whole process, for privacy we need to restrict as much as possible the information available, in order to avoid identification of patients and practitioners by unauthorized users.

The introduction of provenance in a distributed healthcare agent system poses two main risks:

- *cross-link risk*: the risk that unauthorised users are able to link some piece of medical data with an identifiable person by cross-linking information from different sources.
- *event trail risk*: the risk that unauthorised users are able to identify a person by connecting the events and actions related to that person (e.g., the hospitals he has visited in different countries).

Comparing the two risks above, the cross-link risk is more considerable than the event trail risk. In order to identify a person by exploiting the event trail risk, information not available in the healthcare information system (e.g., the places where he lived) has to be matched with the information in the healthcare information system. This requires more effort and information to exploit, than the cross-link risk which can be exploited using information available only in the healthcare information system. For these reasons, our current focus is on the cross-link risk.

In the provenance aware OTMA system we applied two techniques to protect privacy, mainly to reduce the cross link risk: a) we do not store sensitive medical data in the provenance store, and b) we use anonymised patient identifiers in provenance stores. Both of these are supported by the process documentation integration method described in the previous section.

In order to hide medical data from cross-linking, agents do not store sensitive medical data in the provenance store, but only references to such data. This way the provenance store contains only the linkage and the skeleton of the provenance of the medical data, and the healthcare data can be laid on the skeleton by retrieving it from the healthcare information system when needed. The retrieval is done via the EHCR system which is completely under the control of EHCR access rules. With this approach we keep the same degree of privacy of medical data as in the original agent system.

One might think that if we do not store medical information about patients in the provenance store, then no medical information can be inferred about the patient and there is no need to anonymise the patients. However even the fact that the patient was treated can be sensitive information, because the reference to the place where the medical data of the treatment was carried out may contain sensitive information. Such information can be sensitive, because the type of institution can reveal the type of medical intervention, or even the fact that the patient was treated must be treated as part of privacy. Therefore the patient identity has to be anonymised.

The anonymisation procedure should be irreversible: nobody should be able to tell the real identity of the patient by knowing the anonymised identifier. In addition to the anonymisation algorithm mentioned above, the irreversibility is supported by the provenance documentation integration method described in Section 6. The provenance documentation method supports irreversibility of the anonymisation by the way data storage is organized: the anonymisation service does not store the mapping from the real patient identifier to the anonymised patient identifier and computes the anonymised identifier each time it is needed using its own non-trivial algorithm. As a result, the real identifier and the anonymised identifier are not stored together anywhere in the system and the mapping from one identifier to the other cannot be found out without the algorithm of the anonymisation service.

8. Conclusions

In this chapter, we have discussed the important issues of making healthcare agent applications provenance-aware. Provenance-awareness enables users to trace how a particular result has been produced by identifying the individual and aggregated services that produced a particular output. This helps users to get an integrated view of the treatment process executed by distributed autonomous agents, and to be able to carry out audits of the system to assess that, for a given patient, the proper decisions were made and the proper procedures were followed. We discussed the special techniques needed in agent systems to make the autonomous and independent actors provenance aware and produce joint process documentation. We presented provenance awareness through the example of the OTMA agent system in the organ transplant management application domain. We detailed a method of documenting processes by weakly connected autonomous healthcare agents and showed how this method helps to retain security and privacy of data within the process documentation produced by the agent-mediated healthcare system.

In summary, by transforming OTMA into a provenance-aware application, we augmented OTMA with a capability to produce at execution-time an explicit representation of the process actually taking place. Such representation can be then queried and analysed in order to extract valuable information to validate, e.g., the decisions taken in a given case, or to make an audit of the system over a period of time. Making the EHCR system provenance-aware provided a way to have a unified view of a patient's medical record with its provenance (i.e., to connect each part of the medical record with the processes in the real world that originated it and/or the individuals, teams or units responsible for each piece of data).

There are other approaches in literature which are related to provenance. In those first investigations which started to record the origin and history of a piece of data, the concept was called lineage. In the SDTS standard, lineage was a kind of audit trail that traced each step in sourcing, moving, and processing data, mainly related to a single data item, a logical data record, a subset of a database, or to an entire database [11]. There was also relationship to versioning [2] and data warehouses [15]. The provenance concept was later further explored within the GriPhyN project. The application of provenance in grid systems was extended in two respects: 1) data was not necessarily stored in databases and the operations used to derive data items might have been arbitrary computations; and 2) issues relating to the automated generation and scheduling of the computations required to instantiate data products were also addressed. The PROVENANCE project builds on these concepts to conceive and implement an industrial strength open provenance architecture.

To our knowledge, the application of provenance techniques to agent-mediated distributed healthcare applications is novel. In organ allocation management, there are few ICT solutions giving powerful support to the allocation of human organs which keep records of the distributed execution of processes. The EUROTRANSPLANT system is a centralized system where all information and decisions are made in a central server, and all activity is recorded in standard logging systems. The OTM system of Calisti et al. [7] is a distributed system (developed in collaboration with Swisstransplant) which combines agent technology and constraint satisfaction techniques for decision making support in organ transplant centers. In this case all activity is also recorded in standard logging systems.

Acknowledgment

This work has been funded mainly by the IST-2002-511085 PROVENANCE project. Javier Vázquez-Salceda's work has been also partially funded by the "Ramón y Cajal" program of the Spanish Ministry of Education and Science. All the authors would like to thank the PROVENANCE project partners for their inputs to this work.

More information

More information about the IST-2002-511085 EU PROVENANCE project can be found on the project website:

http://twiki.gridprovenance.org/

References

[1] Southampton provenance infrastructure. http://twiki.gridprovenance.org/bin/view/SotonProvenance/WebHome, 2007.

[2] G. Cobena A. Marian, S. Abiteboul and L. Mignet. Change-centric management of versions in an xml warehouse. In *Proc. 27th Int. Conf. of Very Large Data Bases, (VLDB 2001), P. M. G. Apers et al., eds.*, pages 581–590. Morgan Kaufmann, 2001.

[3] F. Bellifemine. *JADE*. CSELT, http://sharon.cselt.it/projects/jade/, 1999.

[4] CEN/TC251 WG I. *Health Informatics-Electronic Healthcare Record Communication- Part 1: Extended architecture and domain model, Final Draft prENV13606-1*, 1999.

[5] The Foundation for Intelligent Phisical Agents, http://www.fipa.org/. *FIPA Specifications*, 2000.

[6] P. Groth, S. Jiang, S. Miles, S. Munroe, V. Tan, S. Tsasakou, and L. Moreau. An architecture for provenance systems. Technical report, Electronics and Computer Science, University of Southampton, October 2006. Available at http://eprints.ecs.soton.ac.uk/12023/.

[7] S. Biellmann M. Calisti, P. Funk and T. Bugnon. A multi-agent system for organ transplant management. in Applications of Software Agent Technology in the Health Care Domain, 2003.

[8] S. Miles, P. Groth, M. Branco, and L. Moreau. The requirements of using provenance in e-science experiments. *Journal of Grid Computing*, 5:1–25, 2007.

[9] S. Munroe, S. Miles, L. Moreau, and J. Vázquez-Salceda. Prime: A software engineering methodology for developing provenance-aware applications. In *Proceedings of the Software Engineering and Middleware Workshop (SEM 2006)*, page 8 pages. ACM Digital, 2006. Published electronically by ACM Digital at http://portal.acm.org/toc.cfm?id=1210525.

[10] J.L. Nealon and ed. A. Moreno. *Applications of Software Agent Technology in the Health Care Domain*. Birkhäuser Verlag, 2003.

[11] S. Khanna P. Buneman and W.-C. Tan. Why and where: A characterization of data provenance. In *Proc. 8th Int. Conf. on Database Theory, (ICDT 2001), LNCS 1973, J. Van den Bussche, V. Vianu, eds.*, pages 316–331. Springer-Verlag, 2001.

[12] J. Vázquez-Salceda, U. Cortés, and J. Padget. Formalizing an electronic institution for the distribution of human tissues. *Artificial Intelligence in Medicine*, 23 (3):233–258, March 2003.

[13] J. Vázquez-Salceda, U. Cortés, J. Padget, A. López-Navidad, and F. Caballero. The organ allocation process: a natural extension of the carrel agent mediated electronic institution. *AI Communications*, 16 (3):153–165, 2003.

[14] S. Willmott, F. O. Fernández Peña, C. Merida Campos, I. Constantinescu, J. Dale, and D. Cabanillas. Adapting agent communication languages for semantic web service inter-communication. In *The 2005 IEEE/WIC/ACM International Con-ference on Web Intelligence (WI'05), Compigne, France, September 2005*, pages 405–408. IEEE Computer Society, 2005.

[15] J. Widom Y. Cui and J.L. Wiener. Tracing the lineage of view data in a warehousing environment. *ACM Transactions on Database Systems*, 25:179–227, 2000.

Javier Vázquez-Salceda and Sergio Álvarez
Universitat Politècnica de Catalunya
Campus Nord UPC, Edifici OMEGA
Jordi Girona 1-3
08034, Barcelona
Spain
e-mail: jvazquez@lsi.upc.edu
      salvarez@lsi.upc.edu

Tamás Kifor and László Z. Varga
Computer and Automation Research Institute
Kende u. 13-17
1111 Budapest
Hungary
e-mail: tamas.kifor@sztaki.hu
      laszlo.varga@sztaki.hu

Simon Miles
Department of Computer Science
King's College London Strand
London WC2R 2LS
United Kingdom
e-mail: simon.miles@kcl.ac.uk

Luc Moreau
School of Electronics and Computer Science
University of Southampton
Southampton SO17 1BJ
United Kingdom
e-mail: L.Moreau@ecs.soton.ac.uk

Steven Willmott
Universitat Politècnica de Catalunya
Campus Nord UPC, Edifici OMEGA
Jordi Girona 1-3
08034, Barcelona
Spain
e-mail: steve@lsi.upc.edu

Whitestein Series in Software Agent Technologies, 65–93
© 2007 Birkhäuser Verlag Basel/Switzerland

Argumentation-Based Agents to Increase Human Organ Availability for Transplant

Pancho Tolchinsky, Ulises Cortés and Dan Grecu

Abstract. In this chapter we describe the work done in the EU project AS-PIC: Argumentation Service Platform with Integrated Components. The main goals of which were 1) to develop a solid theoretical ground for the Argumentation Theory in Artificial Intelligence; 2) based on the theoretical work, develop practical-software components that embody standards for the argumentation-based technology (*inference*, *decision-making*, *dialogue* and *learning*); and *3*) In order to test these components develop two large scale demonstrators. One of these large scale demonstrator is motivated on a medical problem. In particular, how to increase human organ availability for transplantation. It is this medical large scale demonstrator that we focus on in this chapter.

Keywords. ASPIC, Argumentation, Multi-Agent Systems, Health-Care.

1. Introduction

Argumentation has long established itself as an important method of reasoning and interaction between humans. Its use in every day life and in specialised domains such as law and philosophy has led to a variety of argumentation models and has constantly widened the range of problems where it is being applied. The considerable practical benefits of using argumentation in contexts as diverse as inference, decision-making and dialogue, has drawn increasing attention from the computational research community. As a result, recent years have witnessed the emergence of formal models which aim to set argumentation on a rigorous computational basis intended to enable the development of automated computational capabilities built on argumentation

There are two important reasons for which the field of Artificial Intelligence (AI) has devoted a lot of efforts in modelling argumentation: First, argumentation is part of the wider scope of essential cognitive activities in which humans engage, and which AI is keen to model. Second, argumentation lends itself to modelling approaches relying on logic and knowledge representation which are now part of the established set of AI tools. If managed adequately by machines, argumentation has the appeal of a shared method which both humans and computers can employ and which could conceivably support rich forms of interaction and collaboration. This potential of enlisting argumentation in key applications and in human-computer collaboration has ultimately created a need for investigating how argumentation models could be embedded into widely acceptable, usable and effective computational services.

In 2004 a collaboration project funded under the EU Framework Programme 6 has set out to contribute to this objective by proposing a research agenda into theoretical models and requirements for argumentation and by further proposing to develop an Argumentation Services Platform with Integrated Components (AS-PIC). Over nearly 4 years, the ASPIC research consortium has integrated the work of 7 universities and research labs and 2 commercial partners towards the development of theoretical models, the testing of prototypes and the implementation of generic components and services aiming to demonstrate that argumentation is ready to extend from an abstract and formal level to a level where it has immediate and wide-ranging application potential.

In the following pages we will describe and illustrate the benefits of the AS-PIC technology in an area of particular high-value and high-complexity - eHealth. Argumentation is central to medical reasoning as the formulation and evaluation of evidence is present in any medical diagnosis, interpretation of results and in medical assessment processes in general. Therefore, ASPIC has chosen to develop a medical demonstrator to demonstrate the potential and the reach of argumentation technology in a domain of stringent need and considerable potential benefit: the assessment of the viability of human organs for transplants.

The next sections will take the reader on a journey from the intuitive notion of argumentation to the architecture of the CARREL$^+$ application – an agent-based system designed to help geographically-dispersed transplant physicians to deliberate over donor organ viability, and to increase the chances of finding organs satisfying the constraints of the patients awaiting transplants. We will first introduce the reader to the general argumentation background of the ASPIC project and to the relevant contributions of ASPIC in supporting the development of argumentation-based applications. We will then describe in more detail two of the generic argumentation components developed by ASPIC for inference and dialogue. The second half of this chapter will then describe in details how argumentation-based inference and dialogue have supported the development of the CARREL$^+$ agent system for organ transplant mediation.

2. Argumentation and ASPIC

The past few years have seen the emergence of a variety of models for argumentation. One of the main objectives of the ASPIC project was to survey these models and to develop a consensus framework for argumentation which provides generality, is scalable and lends itself to an effective implementation into software components.

Inference is the core element of argumentation which in turn can support other important computational capabilities such as decision-making and dialogue. Therefore theoretical research in ASPIC has devoted a significant amount of effort to the formulation of a widely applicable inference model which lends itself to an effective transition into software. The ASPIC inference model extends the Dung argumentation formalism [5] which develops an argumentation calculus based on the opposition (attack relation) between arguments.

To provide an intuitive illustration of argumentation in ASPIC, let us consider the following set of premises

$$\{a, c\}$$

and the following set of rules

$$\{a \supset b, c \supset d, b \wedge d \supset e\}$$

Here "$\supset$" represents material implication. The inference rule being used is *classical modus ponens*: $x, x \supset y \rightarrow y$

In this context we can state that claim b can be inferred from premise a using rule $a \supset b$ and we write:

$$((a, a \supset b), b)$$

In general, we can write

$$((premises, rule), claim)$$

Meaning that the *claim* can be inferred from the given *premises* using the specified *rule*.

By allowing premises themselves to be inferred, we can develop complex tree-based argument structures. For example, we can build the following argument structure for claim e:

$$((((a, a \supset b), b), ((c, c \supset d), d), b \wedge d \supset e), e)$$

Figure 1 shows the associated argumentation tree, in which the nodes stand for valid premises, and the green arrows represent the rules used to derive claims. The dots on the arrows mark the specific association of the rule with the link relating the premises and the claim.

In the previous examples the inference rules used to construct arguments are taken from classical logic. Different logic formalisms allow us to develop similar constructs with different kinds of premises and/or different kinds of rules. The ASPIC argumentation framework considers two specific types of premises and two types of rules.

Firstly, we distinguish between *premises* which are considered to be *certain* and *assumptions*. In contrast to a premise, an *assumption* is a kind of premise

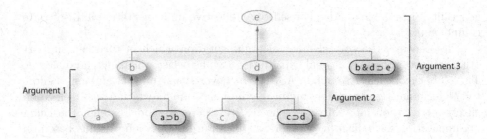

FIGURE 1. Argumentation Tree Example

that could potentially be refuted by counterexamples. This possibility is always relative to a given knowledge base – an assumption in one application may become a certain premise in another (and vice-versa).

Secondly, we distinguish between *strict inference rules* and *defeasible inference rules*. Modus ponens is an example of a strict rule in monotonic logic. Strict rules lead to conclusive inferences which will always remain valid so long as their premises are valid. Defeasible rules, in contrast, are used to define defeasible inferences that could be invalidated in the light of additional information.

To illustrate these distinctions consider the following example. In a 'classical' animal knowledge base, we can consider the premise that "*birds usually fly*" to be an assumption; we are aware that there may be counterexamples of birds that are not flying. We represent this with the formula *bird ↝ flies*.

This is no longer a material implication (in particular, it does not warrant the contraposition: "if it doesn't fly, then it can't be a bird"). So modus ponens is not applicable. Instead, we introduce a defeasible inference rule, called *defeasible modus ponens*:

$$(\varphi, \varphi \rightsquigarrow \psi) \Rightarrow \psi$$

In general, we can construct an argument from a mixture of assumptions and certain premises, using a combination of strict and defeasible rules. In this context, we can make an important distinction that separates argumentation from classical logical inference. We say that an argument is *strict* if it uses only certain premises and strict rules. Otherwise it is *non-strict*.

Broadly, ASPIC operates with two forms of attack: *rebuttal* and *undercutting*:

- Argument A *rebut-attacks* argument B if the claim of A (or any of its intermediate conclusions) directly contradicts the claim of B (or any of its intermediate conclusions). Notice that rebut-attacks are symmetric.
- An argument *undercut-attacks* another argument B by directly contradicting the applicability of B (or any of its sub-arguments).

In order to determine the effects of attacks between arguments, one needs to introduce some grounds for preference between arguments. In ASPIC we have made two primary assumptions about this preference ordering:

1. Any strict argument is preferred to a non-strict argument, and
2. No argument is preferred to a strict argument.

We can now introduce the notion of *defeat*. We shall say that argument A *rebut-defeats* argument B if it rebut-attacks it, and argument B is not preferred to argument A.

Although this gives us the beginnings of a method for resolving conflicts between arguments, it is not sufficient. For example, it is clear that a strict argument can defeat a non-strict argument, but what happens in the case of conflict between non-strict arguments? Argumentation can use various logic formalisms to define attack relations, or to compute argument strengths, which is what lends the ASPIC argumentation model generality. Several such options are further mentioned below.

Using arguments and argument interactions as defined above, the ASPIC formalism proposes methods for evaluating claims in argumentation networks associated with a given knowledge context in order to identify which arguments (and hence their respective claims) are acceptable in some well-defined sense. The answer is to superimpose attack relations over argumentation networks, to propagate their effects through the networks, and to assess the arguments that are defeated. We will call an argumentation network together with its attack/defeat relations an *argumentation framework*.

The ASPIC argumentation framework introduced above has represented the basis for extending the use of argumentation from the realm of logical inference to decision-making, dialogue and machine leaning. One of the ultimate objectives of ASPIC has been to develop generic argumentation-based software components in each of these areas which would transition the computational models evolved in the theoretical segment of the project into services usable in real-life applications. In this context, the ASPIC project has put a special emphasis on enlisting argumentation to support key computational capabilities within intelligent agents. The successful integration of argumentation components with agent architectures has represented one of the most important validation elements of the ASPIC technology, since agents themselves are one of the major carriers of embedded technologies into the real applications field.

The CARREL$^+$ eHealth demonstrator developed by the Polytechnic University of Catalonia has represented one of the two major validation environments of the argumentation technology within the ASPIC project. The CARREL$^+$ agent environment uses argumentation-based inference and dialogue to enable a deliberation between experts relative to the viability of a donor organ for a potential recipient of that organ. CARREL$^+$ uses medical knowledge as input into these deliberation processes and employs agents to mediate between experts situated in remote geographical locations. Given its rich domain background, its complex processing requirements and the criticality of its outputs CARREL$^+$ represents a prime example of using argumentation technology in a real-life operational context.

The following section will prepare the reader for a better understanding of CARREL$^+$ by discussing two of the generic ASPIC argumentation components which play a key role in CARREL$^+$: the Argumentation Engine, which is the AS-PIC argumentation-based inference component, and the Dialogue Manager which is the ASPIC component implemented the argumentation-based dialogue model.

3. The ASPIC Argumentation Engine and Dialogue Manager

3.1. Inference using the Argumentation Engine

The ASPIC inference engine constructs and evaluates the status (accepted or not) of arguments from a defeasible knowledge base for any claim that matches an input query. The ASPIC argumentation framework uses a defeasible model of argument-based inference, consisting of 4 steps:

1. *Argument Construction.*For any claim, arguments are organised into a tree-structure based on a knowledge base K of facts, a set S of strict rules of the form $\alpha_1, ..., \alpha_n \rightarrow \beta$, and a set R of defeasible rules of the form $\alpha_1, ..., \alpha_n \Rightarrow \beta$. The facts are expressed in a language consisting of first order literals and their negations. The ASPIC argumentation framework uses strict and defeasible modus ponens.

2. *Argument Valuation*: Arguments can be assigned a weight. No commitment is made to any particular valuation because the choice of the principle to be used will depend on the application domain.

3. *Argument Interaction*: Once arguments are constructed, binary conflict relations of attack and defeat are defined on this set of arguments. The definition of interactions between arguments depends on the specific logic that is being applied.

4. *Argument Status Evaluation*: Based on the graph of interacting arguments, Dungs calculus of opposition [5] is used to determine the status of arguments, specifically those that are winning or justified.

At the end of this process, a user can view a graphical visualisation of the proof argument network associated with the claim and examine the status, "yes" (accepted) or "no" (not accepted) for each argument. The engine also provides a machine readable version of the proof and results via AIFXML, an XML implementation of the Argument Interchange Format's abstract model [4].

The inferences derivable from a knowledge base can be characterised in terms of the claims of the justified arguments. The key contribution of the ASPIC model is that, in contrast with other approaches to argument-based inference, the model has been demonstrated to satisfy a number of quality postulates [3] which represent a set of minimal requirements that one would require to be satisfied by any rational model of argument based inference.

In the ASPIC model, arguments have at least a claim and numeric support (a real number in the range (0,1]). The support is used to resolve attacks. An atomic argument can be developed from every atomic fact with the fact as the claim and the fact's Degree of Belief (DOB) as the argument's support. Further arguments can be developed through the application of rules. These tree arguments can be valuated with a choice of strategies: weakest link or last link. Weakest link valuation assigns the support for the main argument as the minimum support over all of its sub-arguments. Last link valuation assigns the degree of belief of the highest defeasible rule in the argument tree to the support of the main argument. If there are multiple highest level defeasible rules at the same level in the tree, then it assigns the support of the argument to be the minimum DOB of those rules. As in the underlying knowledge, arguments can be separated into strict and defeasible arguments where a strict argument has a support of 1.0 and a defeasible argument does not.

To define the acceptability of an argument we use defeat relations between all available arguments, and to do that we must define the conflict based attack relation between arguments. Three different types of attack are defined: rebutting, restricted rebutting and undercutting. Literals ~a 0.3. and a 0.5. are both valid and their associated arguments rebut each other. Similarly, an argument formed from the fact a. and the rule b<-a 0.9. rebuts (and is rebutted) by an argument formed from the fact ~b 0.4.. Strict arguments cannot be rebutted. Under restrictive rebutting, an argument whose top rule is strict cannot be rebutted by an argument whose top rule is defeasible.

Every rule in the inference engine knowledge base is automatically associated with a fact its name. The name forms a hidden premise for the rule. A knowledge engineer can explicitly provide that name when the rule is written and then undercut the rule by writing a fact or rule whose head is the contradiction of that name. If argument A undercuts argument B, then A claims that some rule in B is not applicable.

$$A = ((\sim rule\_name) \sim rule\_name) \; ; \; B = ((a, [rule\_name]a \rightsquigarrow b)b)$$

Where $rule\_name$ is the name of the rule $a \rightsquigarrow b$. Note that argument A does not claim b is false, rather, that it cannot be derived from a.

Figure 3 showing a proof network associated with the query "outcome(patient, increase_risk_of_stroke)." The diagram shows one argument (whose main claim is filled in red, defeated) that is developed for the query's claim but then undercut by another argument (whose main claim is filled in green, undefeated). The black arrows in the graph show how sub-arguments are linked together to form a single argument tree. The blue and red arrows in the graph indicate undercut and defeat relations between the two argument trees.

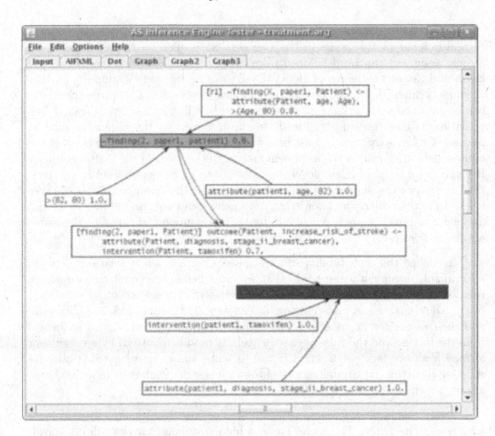

FIGURE 2. A proof network associated with the query, *outcome(patient,increase_risk_of_stroke)*

3.2. Dialogue Using the Dialogue Manager

The ASPIC Dialogue Manager provides a common API for interrogating the state and progress of an argumentation based dialogue. An argumentation based dialogue is characterised by moves whose content consists of claims or arguments that provide an explanation for a particular claim. The API is defined as a series of interfaces that must be implemented by a dialogue component implementation. The ASPIC implementation consists of two parts – a protocol that controls the enactment of the dialogue and a container that acts as an adapter between the protocol and the API. It is envisaged that many protocols can be implemented in this framework. The role of the protocol is to control the initial conditions and the effect of a particular move on the state of a dialogue, e.g., the legal moves, the commitments and the status of the main claim.

The dialogue component expects moves that are constructed with the following attributes:

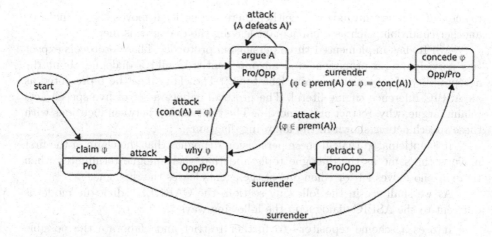

FIGURE 3. Persuasion protocol implemented in the Dialog Component

- agent
- move number
- locution
  - speech act (claim/why/argue/concede/retract)
  - content – a literal or an argument
- target move

In some argumentation based deliberation dialogues the target move is un-needed. In this case it can remain null.

The API consists of interfaces that enable consuming software to establish:

- the dialogue protocol
- the dialogue participants
- the dialogue topic
- the dialogue status (*initialising, in progress, terminated* or *abandoned*)
- the moves that have been previously made
- the commitments of each agent
- the legal moves
- the illegal moves and
- the status of the main claim (*undefeated* or *defeated*)

Each dialogue is represented by an instance of a dialogue object. When it is first created it has status "initialising". In this status, no moves can be made and the protocol, participants and topic must be set. The protocol has built in constraints on the number and role of participants and the topic content. If the protocol/participants and topic are set, and the protocol validates these properties then the dialogue status can be progressed to "in progress". After the dialogue has moved to "in progress", the protocol, participants and topic cannot be changed and the dialogue will proceed as a series of moves (validated by the protocol, and rejected if they are invalid) until either there are no legal moves left to make or another condition, such as a participant leaving the dialogue, is met.

ASPIC has implemented three persuasion protocols. These protocols expect two participants, a proponent and an opponent, to build a dialogue about the acceptability of a particular claim (the topic). The claim must be represented as an ASPIC inference engine literal. The protocol defines a set of five speech acts (claim, argue, why, retract and concede). The relationship between locutions with these speech acts is shown in the following diagram.

It is anticipated that in these persuasion dialogues that the claim of the first move is the same as the dialogue topic and that the dialogue terminates when there are no moves left or when one of the agents leaves the dialogue.

As we shall see in the following section, the CARREL$^+$ dialogue model is different to the ASPIC dialogue in the following ways:

- It uses a scheme repository to further restrict and elaborate the possible attacks on an argument and thus the legal moves.
- It evaluates the defeat relations between argument's using the a number of knowledge resources, such as the reputation of the agents.

In architectural terms, the Carrel Mediator agent exposes the same interface as the ASPIC dialogue component but must expose interfaces for managing the scheme repository and the evaluation component. At the moment the CARREL$^+$ evaluation components is seen as a separate entity to the interaction evaluation module within the inference engine that is consumed by the dialogue component, but it is hoped that in later iterations that these two layers can be shared.

4. Human Organ Transplantation and CARREL$^+$

Human organ transplantation constitutes the only effective therapy for many life-threatening diseases. However, while the increasing success of transplants has led to increase in demand, the lack of a concomitant increase in donor organ availability has led to a growing disparity between supply and demand. Nonetheless, in spite organ scarcity, an important number of human organs, available for transplantation, are discarded as being considered to be non-viable (not suitable) for that purpose. It has been acknowledged [6] that these discard rates can be reduced if one accounts for two factors that are currently not taken into account in the current organ selection process: 1), doctors often disagree as to whether an organ is viable, and different hospitals and regions have different policies; 2)organs are rarely viable or non-viable per se, but rather assessment of viability should depend on both the donor and potential recipient characteristics, as well as for courses of action to be undertaken during transplantation

We propose a novel organ selection process that uses a multi-agent system called CARREL$^+$ to let geographically dispersed transplant physicians deliberate over organ viability and, in that way, help increase the availability of organs for transplantation.

4.1. The CARREL$^+$ System

Since 1980 the number of transplant requests has been constantly increasing. Hence, human transplant coordinators are currently facing significant problems in dealing with the workload involved in the management of requests, and assignation and distribution of tissues and organs. Moreover, the demand for organs and tissues are expected to continue to rise and lead to ever increasing demands on transplant coordinators. Furthermore, the scarcity of donors has led to the creation of national and international coalitions of transplant organizations. This has resulted in requirements for managing and processing vast and complex data, and accommodation of a complex set of regulations. Hence, in [12] an agent-based architecture – CARREL – is proposed for efficient management of the data to be processed in carrying out recipient selection, organ and tissue allocation, ensuring adherence to legislation, following approved protocols and preparing delivery plans. In order to perform these tasks CARREL is required to manage and process vast and complex data, as well as to adhere to complex, in some cases conflicting, sets of national and international regulations and protocols governing exchange of organs and tissues. This has motivated development of CARREL, an electronic institution that encodes sets of legislation and protocols based on two physical institutions representing examples of best practice: the OCATT (Organització CATalana de Trasplantaments)[1] and ONT (Organización Nacional de Transplantes)[2] organ transplantation organizations for Catalonia and Spain respectively.

The Spanish model has two organizational levels:

Intra-hospital:: Where the role of a hospital Transplant Coordinator has been created to improve the coordination of all those involved at any step of the donor procurement, allocation and transplantation process.

Inter-hospital:: Where an intermediary organization (OCATT for Catalonia and ONT for the whole of Spain) was created to improve the communication and coordination of all the participating health-care transplant organizations.

Figure 4a. illustrates the inter-hospital level managed by CARREL, and entities interacting with CARREL. The ONT and OCATT denote the organ transplantation organizations that *own* the agent platform and act as observers. Each UCTx denotes a transplant coordination unit representing a hospital associated to CARREL. Each UCTx manages the intra-hospital level; its goal being to successfully bring to completion the organ and tissue procurement, extraction and implantation processes. Each UCTx is in turn modelled as an agency.

The role of the CARREL Institution includes the following tasks:

T1 to ensure that all the agents that enter into the institution follow the behavioral norms.

T2 to remain informed of all the recipients that are registered in the waiting lists.

---

[1] http://www10.gencat.net/catsalut/ocatt/en/htm/index.htm
[2] http://www.ont.es

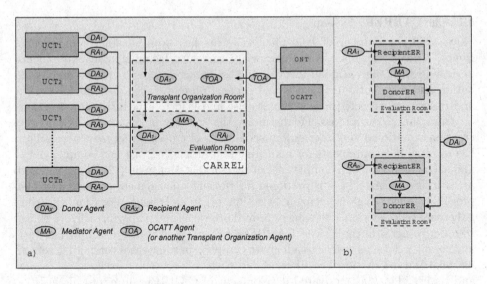

FIGURE 4. a) CARREL extended with the two additional rooms in order to manage the new selection process. b) The MA coordinating the proponent agents' deliberations in the Evaluation Rooms

T3 to check that all hospitals fulfill all the requirements needed to interact with CARREL.

T4 to coordinate the piece delivery from one facility to another.

T5 to register all incidents relating to a particular piece.

A hospital becomes a member of the CARREL institution in order to make use of the services provided. In doing so, they undertake an obligation to respect the norms ruling interactions inside CARREL. For example:

N1 All organ offers and tissue requests should be done through CARREL.

N2 Hospitals must accept the outcomes of the assignation process.

N3 Hospitals must update CARREL with any relevant event related to organs and tissues received from the Institution.

In [9] an extension to CARREL, CARREL$^+$, is proposed to support an alternative selection process intended to help reduce the number of discarded organs.

CARREL is a type of dialogical system in which all interactions are compositions of message exchanges, or illocutions, structured through agent group meetings called scenes or rooms. Each agent can be associated with one or more roles, and these roles define the rooms the agent can enter and the protocols it should follow. Thus, extending CARREL involves defining new roles and/or new illocutions, where the former may imply defining new rooms. It is worth noting that CARREL makes no assumptions about the internal reasoning models of the participant agents or the resources referenced.

For CARREL to support the new human organ selection process we make use of the ASPIC's **dialogue** and **inference** components as well as of the argument-based model *ProCLAIM* [11]. This model defines a setting for *proponent* agents (e.g., donor and recipient agents, agents representing the donor and the recipient resp.) to argue over the appropriateness of their intended decisions. The model features a Mediator Agent that directs these proponent agents in their deliberation and subsequently evaluates the submitted arguments so as to conclude whether a proposed decision is appropriate (e.g., whether the organ is viable or not). Hence, the main extension in CARREL$^+$ is the inclusion of the Mediator Agent (MA) role for managing the donor and recipient agents deliberation over the viability of an available organ. As depicted in figure 4 the agents' deliberation takes place in two new scenes: the *Donor Evaluation Room* and *Recipient Evaluation Room*.

4.2. The Human Organs Selection and Assignation Process

The human organ selection process illustrates the ubiquity of disagreement and conflict of opinion in the medical domain. What may be a sufficient reason for discarding an organ for some qualified professionals may not be for others. Different policies in different hospitals and regions exist, and a consensus among medical professionals is not always feasible. Hence, contradictory conclusions may be derived from the same set of facts. For example, suppose a donor with a smoking history of more than 20-30 packs a year and no history of *chronic obstructive pulmonary disease* (COPD). The medical guidelines indicate that a donor's smoking history is a sufficient reason for deeming a donor's lung as non-viable [8]. However, there are qualified physicians that reason that the donor's lung is viable given that there is no history of COPD [6]. Similarly, the guidelines suggest discarding the kidney of a donor whose cause of death was *streptococcus viridans endocarditis* (*sve*)[8]. However, some reason that by administrating *penicillin* to the recipient the kidney can safely be transplanted.

The human organ selection process begins when a potential donor becomes available. The donor's organs deemed non-viable by the Transplant Coordinator (which we name the Donor Agent, DA) are discarded, whereas the organs deemed viable are offered via a third-party (Transplant Organization) in a queue to Transplant Units, (which we name Recipient Agents) that may be located in different hospitals. These Recipient Agents, $RA_1,...,RA_n$, to which the organ may eventually be offered, in which case, if they accept the organ, they may attempt to implant it to a potential recipient they are responsible for. Or, if every RA_j fails to accept the organ, it is discarded, i.e., not extracted from the donor.

A DA's decision to not offer an organ which he believes to be non-viable prevents other RA_j's from having the opportunity to make use of that organ. We propose an alternative selection process managed by CARREL$^+$. In this alternative process a DA_i that detects a potential donor offers all the potentially transplantable organs irrespective of whether he believes the organs to be viable or non-viable. CARREL$^+$ then distributes the offer to the appropriate RAs.

When there is a match between the offered organ and a potential recipient the DA_i and the appropriate RA_j are informed of this match and of the clinical data made available by these agents of the donor and potential recipient. On the basis of this data the agents inform CARREL$^+$ on whether they believe the organ to be viable or not. If they agree, the organ is deemed viable or not in accordance with the agents' decision. However id disagree, an argument-based dialogue take place between DA_i and RA_j to decide whether the organ is or is not viable. In particular, a DA_i's arguments for the non-viability of an organ may now be defeated by the RA_j's arguments for viability, and thus, RA_j may have the opportunity to make use of that organ. In the same way, DA_i's arguments for the viability of the offered organ may be stronger than those of a RA_j for non-viability, thus, making RA_j reconsider.

In the following section we describe the ASPIC's medical large scale demonstrator.

5. The ASPIC's Medical Large Scale Demonstrator

In order to demonstrate the use of the ASPIC components two large scale demonstrators were developed. The medical and the business large scale demonstrators. The former aims to test the use of the inference an dialogue components in a complex scenario as the human organ transplantation. The latter demonstrator aims to test the use of the inference, decision making and learning components in a somewhat simpler scenario (a central business has to decide whether clients' requests to increase their credit should be accepted). This demonstrator deals with large databases and number of clients which allow testing other aspects of the AS-PIC components, e.g., speed performance, performance with an increasing number of client requests, etc...

We now discus the medical demonstrator's architecture to later illustrate its functionalities through an example.

The starting point is a framework consisting of a DA and a RA directed by the dialogue component in the exchange of arguments constructed using the inference component (see fig. 5). However, given the critical nature of decision to be taken, a richer framework is required to ensure that the dialogue is focused on the subject matter, that the agents' arguments and final decision comply with the medical guidelines, while accounting to previous similar dialogues (and thus to the evidence in the correctness of previous similar decisions) as well as to the agents' reputation that allows the flexibility in the decision-making required in this domain[3]. These aspects are addressed by the *ProCLAIM* model developed within the ASPIC project.

---

[3]Transplant organizations periodically publish the consented organ acceptability criteria. However, these criteria rapidly evolve because of the researchers' effort in extending them to reduce organ discards. Hence, the more advanced transplant units deviate from consented criteria.

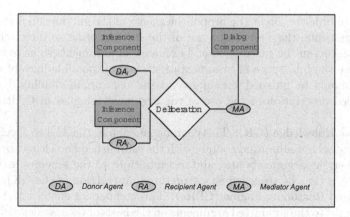

FIGURE 5. Basic Argument-Based Framework for Deliberating
Over the Viability of a Human Organ

5.1. The *ProCLAIM* Model

Broadly construed, the *ProCLAIM* model consist of a mediator agent (MA) direct-ing *proponent* agents in an argument based deliberation, in which the final decision should comply with certain domain dependent guidelines (e.g., the medical criteria for accepting a donor's organ for transplantation). However, the arguments sub-mitted by the proponent agents may persuade the MA to accept decisions that deviate from the guidelines. For example, the MA may be able to reason that the submitted arguments supporting an alternative decision have proven to be correct in previous similar deliberations.

ProCLAIM defines three main tasks for the MA: 1) Inform the proponent agents as to what are their dialectical possible moves at each stage of the delib-eration; 2) Ensure that the submitted arguments are relevant (*e.g.*, comply with the guidelines), and *3)* Evaluate the submitted arguments in order to identify the *winning* arguments and thus determine whether a proposed decision is justified. This last task may require the assignment of strengths to the given arguments and possibly submission of additional arguments. In order to undertake these tasks, MA references four knowledge resources (see fig. 6):

Argument Scheme Repository (ASR): The ASR encodes a structured set of argument schemes and their associated critical questions (CQ) [13]. These schemes embody stereotypical patterns of reasoning. Instantiations of argu-ment schemes can be seen as providing a justification in favour of the conclu-sion of the argument. The instantiated scheme (what we term an 'argument') can be questioned (attacked) through posing critical questions associated with the scheme. Each critical question can itself be posed as an attacking argument instantiating a particular scheme. This scheme is then itself subject to critical questioning.

In order to direct the proponent agents in the submission and exchange of arguments, the MA makes use of the ASR in order to direct the proponent agents in the submission and exchange of arguments so as to effectively explore the full 'space of argumentation', i.e., all possible lines of reasoning that should be pursued w.r.t a given issue, e.g., organ viability. For a more detailed description of the use of the argument schemes in CARREL$^+$ see [10].

Guideline Knowledge (GK): This component enables the MA to check whether the arguments submitted comply with the established knowledge, by checking whether the arguments are valid instantiations of the schemes in ASR (the ASR can thus be regarded as a structured abstraction of the GK).

Case-Based Reasoning Engine (CBRe): This component enables MA to assign strengths to the submitted arguments on the basis of their associated evidence gathered from past deliberations, as well as provide additional arguments deemed relevant in previous similar situations (see [11]).

Argument Source Manager (ASM): Depending on the source from whom the arguments are submitted, the strengths of these arguments may be readjusted by the MA. Thus, this component manages the knowledge related to, for example, the agents' roles and/or reputations.

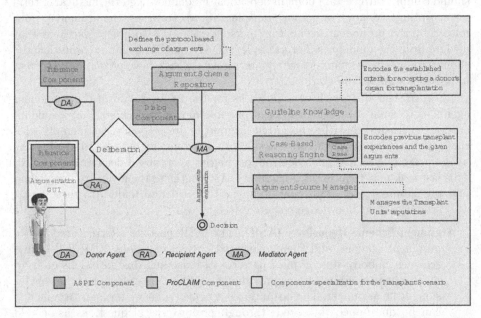

FIGURE 6. Argument-Based Framework for Deliberating Over the Viability of a Human Organ using the ASPIC components and the *ProCLAIM* model.

In the transplantation context, the GK encodes medical knowledge relevant to assessing the viability of an organ, and the ASR encodes the stereotypical reasoning patterns used in deliberating over the viability of an organ. The CBR component allows for evaluation of the agents' submitted arguments on the basis of previous similar transplant experiences. Finally, the ASM manages the agents' reputations. The latter is in fact modeled as a *trusted third party's* (the National Transplant Organizations) assessment as to what degree of deviation from the established criteria should be allowed for each transplant unit, i.e., each donor and recipient agent.

Currently the implementation of the dialogue component and the CBR component require readjustments. This is because while the dialogue component requires to resolve the strength of an argument as this is submitted, for the CBR to assign strength to the arguments it requires the full dialogue graph (see [11]), and thus, the MA can derive if an argument is or is not sufficiently strong on the basis of previous dialogues only when all the arguments where submitted.

Note that *ProCLAIM* makes no assumptions about the internal reasoning mechanisms of the proponent agents (e.g., DA and RA). This allows for human agents to construct natural language arguments instantiating schemes, or automated agents constructing arguments in a first order logic programming language. These two options are explored in the ASPIC implementation that we now discus.

5.2. The Agents' Implementation

Three agents are featured in the ASPIC medical demonstrator. The donor and recipient agents and a mediator agent. All three agents are implemented in jade[4] and thus interact in a jade platform.

5.2.1. The Mediator Agent.
The MA is implemented as a semi-autonomous agent where only few tasks, that we now describe, are delegated to a human user via MA's GUI.

Figure 7 shows the MA's GUI, where a user can see at each time the exchanged messages (top panel), the available legal moves (mid panel) and the argument-based dialogue moves (below panel). Note that moves in blue are undefeated arguments, moves in red are defeated arguments and moves in black are moves that are not arguments (*why*, *concede* or *retract* moves).

We can also see that the user can load a Guideline Knowledge, an ASR and a knowledge base of agents' reputation. For consistency in the dialogue, this can only be done before the dialogue starts. Finally the user can terminate a running dialogue at anytime.

The MA has two main tasks: 1) inform the participants of their available moves at each stage of the dialogue; and 2) check whether the participants submitted arguments should be accepted.

The first task involves querying the dialogue manager for the legal moves with respect to the persuasion protocol introduced in section 3.2 and then reference the

---

[4]http://jade.tilab.com/

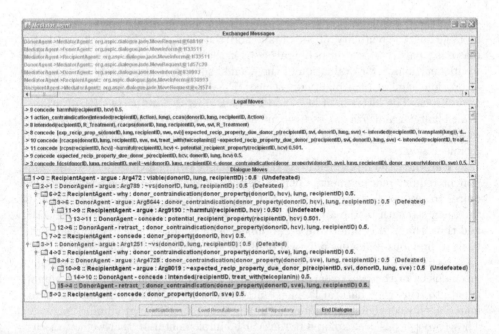

FIGURE 7. Mediator Agent's GUI

ASR to filter these moves to only those that are relevant for arguing over the organ viability. For example, while the dialogue component allows the proponent agent to start with any claim or argue locution (the legal moves are represented as `claim(X)` and `argue(since(X,Y))` being X and Y ungrounded variables representing the claim and support of the argument respectively) the ASR will filter these moves to only arguments that instantiate the argument scheme for the organ viability:

Claim: $viable(Donor, Organ, Recipient)$
Support: $[vs(Donor, Organ, Recipient)] viable(Donor, Organ, Recipient)$
$\Leftarrow available\_organ(Donor, Organ), potential\_recipient(Recipient, Organ).$
$available\_organ(Donor, Organ). potential\_recipient(Recipient, Organ).$

Where $vs(Donor, Organ, Recipient)$ is the name of the defeasible rule $viable(Donor, Organ, Recipient) \Leftarrow available\_organ(Donor, Organ),$ $potential\_recipient(Recipient, Organ).$

That is, if there is an available organ for a potential recipient it is presumably viable.

The second task, checking whether the participants submitted arguments should be accepted, involves first checking that the submitted move is legal with respect to the dialogue's protocol and the ASR. If it is accepted and the move is not an argument, it is added to the dialogue graph. If the move is an argument further checking is required. The MA has to check that the argument is compliant with the GK. If it is, the argument is accepted (added to the dialogue graph). If it is not accepted by the GK, if the submitter of the argument has sufficiently good reputation the argument may still be accepted, under the condition that the user validates this decision, as illustrated in figure 8.

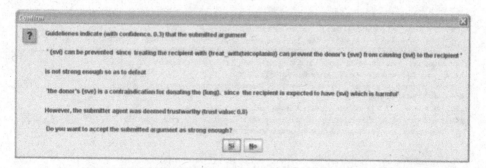

FIGURE 8. Dialogue window that the MA's user has to confirm for exceptionally accepting an argument not validated by the guidelines but which submitter has good reputation

5.2.2. The Donor Agent. The DA is conceived as an autonomous agent able to reason about the incoming dialogue moves, as well as construct and submit new moves in a logic programming language for which it uses the ASPIC inference component.

The DA has a GUI (see figure 9) where the user can view the agent's exchanged messages, the argument-based dialogue moves, the DA's intended moves, the DA's moves that where sent, accepted and rejected by the MA. The agent's GUI also allows the user to load at anytime an alternative knowledge base, or to load new knowledge (fact or rule) as depicted in figure 10. As we will see in the example introduced in section 5.3 new knowledge can change the agent's beliefs so as to, for example, retract from previously made dialogue moves.

The DA does not yet implements a method for deciding when to withdraw from dialogue. Hence this is done by the user (if no other agent has terminated the dialogue previously). With the sole purpose of controlling the demo's timing, it is the DA's user that decides when each of the agent's intended moves is to be submitted. This does not affect any relevant aspect of the DA's reasoning.

Finally, the DA's gui allows offering a new organ introducing the donor and organ characteristics as displayed in figure 11.

5.2.3. The Recipient Agent. As illustrated in figure 6, the RA is conceived as a user (medical doctor) interacting with a decision support system (DSS) that beneath has a proxy agent that communicates with the MA. The DSS assists the user in retrieving the submitted moves allowing the user to make only moves that

FIGURE 9. Donor Agent's GUI

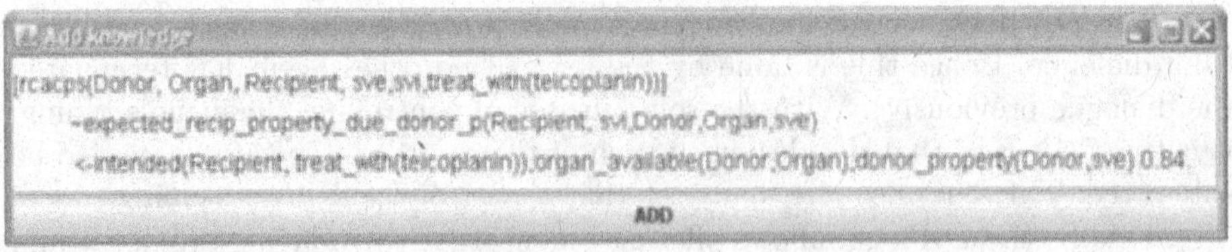

FIGURE 10. Dialogue window to add new knowledge to a *DA* or a *RA*

are legal from the viewpoint of the protocol and the ASR (i.e., the legal moves facilitated by the *MA*). The DSS is integrated with the ASPIC inference component

FIGURE 11. Dialogue windows to make an organ offer (left) and
to update CARREL$^+$ of a new potential recipient (right)

that enables the DSS recommend dialogue moves with which to reply to previously submitted move. While the DA construct arguments in logic programming language, the user does so in pseudo-natural language. In particular, as shown in figure 13, arguments are constructed by filling in the blanks in a template and the DSS can suggests possible instantiations compliant with the DSS's knowledge base.

For every selected argument-based move or suggested instantiation the user can call the inference component to display the argument tree (see figure 14) which allows the user to see the rational behind each DSS's recommendation. Such is also the case when a match between organ and potential recipient is found and the RA has to inform CARREL$^+$ on whether the he believes the offered organ is viable or not (see fig 15). The DSS recommends an assessment on the organ viability based on its knowledge base and the user can view the argument graph for such recommendation.

As in the case with the DA, the user can at anytime load an alternative knowledge base or add new knowledge. Finally the DSS allows the user to update information of potential recipients as shown in figure 11.

5.3. Running the Demonstrator

The demo starts with a DA and a RA informing CARREL$^+$ of an available organ and of a potential recipient respectively (see fig 11). As soon as there is a match between an offered organ and a patient in the waiting list both the appropriate DA and RA are informed of this match together with the patient's and donor's clinical data. On the basis of this data the agents inform CARREL$^+$ of whether they believe the organ is viable or not. The DA is an autonomous software agent,

P. Tolchinsky, U. Cortés and D. Grecu

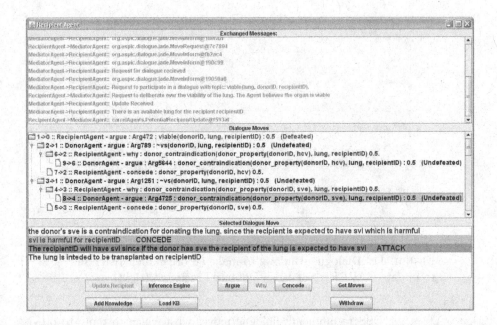

FIGURE 12. Recipient Agent's GUI

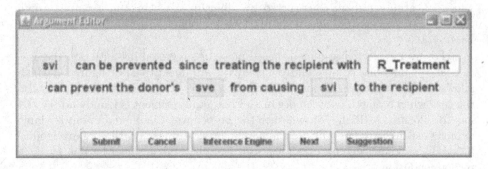

FIGURE 13. The *RA* constructs argument in pseudo-natural language. The user can either request the DSS for a suggestion on how to instantiated the variable R_Treatment or instantiate it himself.

and thus it creates and submits its response automatically. The *RA*'s DSS provides the user with an argument why it should deem the organ as viable or not. The user may accept or reject such suggestion. If both agents agree on the organ viability no deliberation takes place and the organ is deemed viable or non viable by the *MA* in accordance with the *DA* and *RA* assessment. If they disagree, the *MA* uses the dialogue component to initiate a new dialogue instance where the agent that

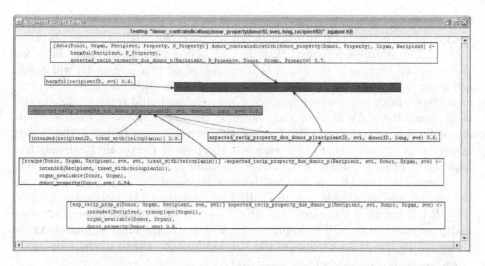

FIGURE 14. A proof network associated with the query, *donor_contraindication(donor_property(donorID,sve),lung,recipientID)*. The claim is defeated, namely, *sve* is not deemed as a contraindication because the infection on the recipient can be prevented.

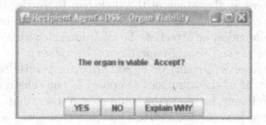

FIGURE 15. Dialogue window asking for confirmation from the *RA*'s user on the assessment of the offered organ's viability

believes the organ to be viable undertake the proponent's role and the other the opponent's. The dialogue protocol is set to be the persuasion protocol introduced in section 3.2 and the topic of the dialogue is set to: `viable(donorID,organ, recipientID)`, with `donorID` being the donor identification, `organ` is the offered organ and `recipientID` is the potential recipient's identification.

The first move in the dialogue is the argument for viability. This argument is submitted by the *MA* on behalf of the proponent agent. Subsequent moves will attack or defend this argument.

Let us suppose the *DA* offers a lung of a donor, `donorID`, whose cause of death was a streptococcus viridans endocarditis (`donor_property(donorID,sve)`) and had hepatitis C (`donor_property(donorID,hcv)`), as illustrated in figure 11.

Let as supposes as well that the offer arrives to a RA responsible for the patient
`recipientID` (figure 11) that although not reported to CARREL$^+$, has also hepatitis C. Let us suppose as well that the DA believes the lung is not viable for
`recipientID` because if the organ is transplanted to this patient he will result
in having: 1) an infection caused by the streptococcus viridans bacteria; and 2)
hepatitis C. Both being severe infections, bacterial and viral respectively. On the
other hand, the RA's DSS suggests deeming the organ as viable because there
are no known contraindications. The bacterial infection can be prevented by administrating teicomplanine to the recipient and patient `recipientID` already has
hepatitis C, hence it cannot be deemed as a harmful consequence of the transplant.

Supposing the DSS persuades the user to deem the organ as viable and
the appropriate message is sent to CARREL$^+$, a dialogue is initiate by the MA
with RA being the proponent, DA the opponent and `viable(donorID,lung,`
`recipientID)` the topic. The argument for viability of the lung (argument A1) is
submitted by the MA on behalf of the RA and broadcasted to the participants.

Claim: $viable(donorID, lung, recipientID)$
Support: $[vs(Donor, Organ, Recipient)]viable(Donor, Organ, Recipient) \Leftarrow$
$available\_organ(Donor, Organ), potential\_recipient(Recipient, Organ).$
$available\_organ(donorID, lung).potential\_recipient(recipientID, lung).$

Together with the submitted move the MA inform the participants of their
available legal moves at this stage of the dialogue. From the view point of the
dialogue protocol, each premise in the argument's support can be conceded, chal-
lenged with a `why` locution or attacked via an argument with claim the negation
of one of the premises (i.e., $\sim vs(Donor, Organ, Recipient)$,
$\sim available\_organ(Donor, Organ)$ or $\sim potential\_recipient(Recipient, Organ))$.
Note that the content of the argument's support is not constraint. To focus the
dialogue on the relevant issues to be addressed, rather than all the logically
possible, the MA references the ASR. Thus, for example, the legal moves to
reply to the argument for viability are reduced to only arguments that claim
$\neg vs(Donor, Organ, Recipient)$ on the basis of, for example, a donor's contraindication, an organ dysfunction or a logistical contraindication. Also the opponent
may concede to $vs(Donor, Organ, Recipient)$ in which the dialogue ends. Note
that the opponent cannot attack the premise $available\_organ(Donor, Organ)$ or
$potential\_recipient(Recipient, Organ)$ nor it can challenge any of the premises of
the argument for viability. Any of these moves would be deemed illegal. In this way
the dialogue is initially focused on whether or not there are any contraindications
for transplanting the available organ.

Amongst the legal moves the MA sends to the opponent agent, in this case
the DA, is the Donor Contraindication Scheme:

Claim: $\neg vs(donorID, lung, recipientID)$
Support: $[dcs(donorID, lung, recipientID, DonorProperty)]$
$\sim vs(donorID, lung, recipientID) \Leftarrow$
$donor\_contraindication(donorID, lung, recipientID, DonorProperty),$

> *donor_property(donorID, DonorProperty).*
> *donor_contraindication(donorID, lung, recipientID, DonorProperty).*
> *donor_property(donorID, DonorProperty).*

Note that the donor the recipient and the organ are know by the context (instantiated by the *MA*) and what reminds to be instantiated by the *DA* is *DonorProperty*. Namely, identify a property on the donor that the *DA* believes to be a contraindication. In this case, the *DA* constructs and submits two arguments, A2 and A3, identifying hepatitis C (*hcv*) and streptococcus viridans endocarditis (*sve*) as contraindications for transplanting the lung.

The submitted arguments are then evaluated by the *MA* to check that they are legal with respect to the dialogue component protocol, the ASR and the Guidelines Knowledge. The latter allows *MA* to check that the argument instantiation is legal, in this case, that *hcv* and *sve* are in fact contraindications.

Supposing these two arguments are accepted by the *MA* and thus added to the dialogue graph, the *MA* will broadcasts the accepted moves together with the legal moves to the participants. At this stage the argument for viability is defeated and so if the dialogue terminates at this point the lung would be deemed nonviable. Hence, to defend the organ's viability the *RA* must defeat both arguments A2 and A3.

The *RA* may request for some evidence on the facts that the donor had *hcv* and *sve* by challenging premises *donor_property(donorID, hcv)* and *donor_property(donorID, sve)* of arguments A2 and A3 respectively. Or, concede these premises relying on *DA*'s information. However, since *RA* does not agree with *donor_contraindication(donorID, lung, recipientID, hcv)* nor *donor_contraindication(donorID, lung, recipientID, sve)* he will try to attack such premises. Legal attacks on these premises are based on 1) the potential recipient is in a highly precarious condition (risk of death in the following 24 hours) that can only be overcome with a lung transplant, hence hcv (sve rep.) cannot be deemed as a contraindication; 2) hcv (resp. sve) is a risk factor of some condition X known to be a contraindication, but the donor does not have X.[5] Neither is the case, so the *RA*'s DSS is unable to construct an attacking argument on either A2 or A3. Therefore, it suggest challenging the facts that *hcv* and *sve* are contraindication, effectively shifting the burden of proof back to *DA*. The user can ask the DSS why the challenge locution is suggested to which the DSS will display an argument attacking *donor_contraindication(donorID, lung, recipientID, sve)* (rep. *hcv*) as depicted in figure 14.

Note that at any time the user may ignore the DSS's suggestions and submit any other dialogue move. Nonetheless, the DSS allows the user submitting only moves that are legal from the viewpoint of the dialogue's protocol and the ASR.

---

[5] An example use of this argument would be to attack the fact that smoking history is a contraindication when the donor does not have chronical obstructive pulmonary disease.

Supposing the RA finally concedes to the facts that the donor had hcv and sve but challenges the fact that these are contraindications, the DA will have to justify why these conditions are contraindication.

Amongst the schemes the DA can instantiate to defend A2 as well as A3 is the Donor Disease Transmit Scheme:

Claim:

$donor\_contraindication(donor\_property(donorID, sve), lung, recipientID)$

Support: $[ddts(donorID, lung, recipientID, sve, R\_Property)]$

$donor\_contraindication(donor\_property(donorID, sve), lung, recipientID)$
$\Leftarrow harmful(recipientID, R\_Property), expected\_recip\_property\_due\_donor$
$\_p(recipientID, R\_Property, donorID, lung, sve).$

$[exp\_recip\_prop\_s(donorID, lung, recipientID, sve, R_{P}roperty)]$

$expected\_recip\_property\_due\_donor\_p(recipientID, R\_Property, donorID,$
$lung, sve) \Leftarrow intended(recipientID, transplant(lung))$
$, donor\_property(donorID, sve). intended(recipientID, transplant(lung)).$
$donor_{p}roperty(donorID, sve). harmful(recipientID, R\_Property).$

The DA can thus instantiate this scheme to indicate that sve (rep. hcv) is a contraindication because the recipient will result having svi: streptococcus viridans infection (resp. hcv) which is harmful.

Supposing these two arguments (A4 and A5 respectively) are submitted by DA and accepted by MA, the RA will have to defeat both A4 and A5 in order to defend the organ's viability. In this case the RA's DSS suggest to attack both arguments indicating in the first case that given that $recipientID$ already has hcv, resulting in having hcv cannot be deemed as a harmful consequence of the transplant. In the latter case, the DSS suggests attack A5 (see figure 12) by arguing that the infection on the recipient can be prevented by administrating teicoplanine to the recipient (see figure 13).

Let us suppose that both arguments (A6 and A7 respectively) are submitted by RA and, that while A6 is validated by MA, MA derives from Guidelines that there is not enough confidence on the use of teicoplanine for the prevention of svi so as to accept argument A7. Let us also suppose that RA has good reputation and thus his assessment that the suggested antibiotic can effectively prevent the recipient's infection may be accepted (see figure 8). If the MA finally accepts both arguments as legal, the status of acceptability of the initial argument would be accepted, i.e., the organ would be deemed viable for $recipientID$.

In this example, when DA is informed of the submission of A6 it updates its knowledge base adding the fact that $recipientID$ already has hcv (it trusts the RA assessment on that matters), in consequence it concedes to the fact that the recipient has hcv and retracts from its previous claim that hcv is a contraindication (see figure 9). In general, at any time new knowledge can be added to an agent's knowledge base that may result in changes in the agent's believes. The dialogue can accommodate to such changes by allowing participants to retract and in general to backtrack to reply to any previously submitted dialogue moves. Another example of this is if we add via the DA's interface new knowledge (see figure 10) indicating that teicoplanine is an effective treatment to prevent svi, the DA will also retract from its claim that sve is a contraindication.

At any point during the dialogue the participant agents can withdraw, or the MA can terminate the dialogue and the resolution is given by the dialectical status of acceptability of the argument for viability, in this case, the argument is accepted and thus, if the dialogue terminates the MA will send both DA and RA a message informing them that the lung was deemed viable for $recipientID$.

6. Conclusions

In this chapter we have described the work done in the ASPIC project focusing on use of the ASPIC's component by the medical large scale demonstrator, CARREL$^+$. A multi-agent institution in which agents argue over the viability of human organs intended for transplantation. In so doing, organs that would ordinarily be discarded may now be successfully transplanted, so reducing the disparity between supply and demand. CARREL$^+$ extends CARREL, an agent-based logistical framework supporting human organ and tissue transplantation. The required argumentation framework is based on the ASPIC's components and the *ProCLAIM* model

Thus the ASPIC component together with the *ProCLAIM* model provide an environment in which: 1) transplant physicians can effectively interchange arguments relevant for the deliberation; 2) software agents can assist physicians in the construction, retrieval and validation of arguments as well as in identifying their valid moves at any stage of the argument-based deliberation; and finally *3)* the submitted arguments *for* and *against* the organ viability can be evaluated on the basis of the established medical criteria while allowing deviation from prestigious transplant units (with good reputation). We are currently working on integrating the CBR in the CARREL$^+$'s argumentation process. This will also allow evaluating the arguments strength on the basis of previous transplant experiences.

Regarding related works, some works have proposed multi-agent approaches for providing support to medical practitioners in the tasks of data management and decision making in the transplant domain (e.g., [2], [7]). As in CARREL, the main objective of these works is to speed-up and reduce the complexity of the tasks involved in the transplant processes. However, these works all assume the current human organ selection process so that an organ is considered as available for transplantation only when the professionals at the donor's site deem the organ to be viable. Otherwise it is simply not offered (discarded). We believe it is crucial to ensure that **all** organs are offered for transplantation if the objective of reducing the disparity between supply and demand is to be achieved. To cope with the added complexity a distributed platform such as CARREL$^+$ is required.

CARREL$^+$ uses schemes and critical questions in order to map out the full space of argumentation w.r.t. viability of organs for transplantation, and in such a way that agents engaged in a argumentation based dialogue will be guided in exploring all their dialectical obligations. It is worth noting that a similar idea has been explored in the context of arguing about (deciding) an appropriate course of action [1]. In order to evaluate whether the schemes and CQ do indeed capture all the required lines of reasoning/argumentation, we are currently working on refining the ASR in collaboration with doctors at the Department of Organ & Tissue Procurement for Transplantation in the Hospital de la Santa Creu i Sant Pau. We have developed an interactive web page[6] from where we receive the doctors' comments on the argument schemes' representation and organization of the ASR. In particular our current concern is to minimize the users' overhead in the interaction with the schemes (instantiating or editing them) while ensuring that these schemes do indeed capture all the needed reasoning patterns.

References

[1] K. M. Atkinson, T. J. M. Bench-Capon, and P. McBurney. A dialogue game protocol for multi-agent argument for proposals over action. In *Proc. First International Workshop on Argumentation in Multi-Agent Systems (ArgMAS 2004)*, 2004.

[2] M. Calisti, P. Funk, S. Biellman, and T. Bugnon. A multi-agent system for organ transplant management. In *Applications of Software Agent Technology in the Health Care Domain, WSSAT*, 2003.

[3] M. Caminada and L. Amgoud. On the evaluation of argumentation formalisms. *Artif. Intell.*, 171(5-6):286–310, 2007.

[4] C. Chesñevar, J. McGinnis, S. Modgil, I. Rahwan, C. Reed, G. Simari, M. South, G. Vreeswijk, and S. Willmott. Towards an argument interchange format. *Knowl. Eng. Rev.*, 21(4):293–316, 2006.

[5] P. M. Dung. On the acceptability of arguments and its fundamental role in non-monotonic reasoning, logic programming and n-person games. *Artificial Intelligence*, 77:321–357, 1995.

[6] A. López-Navidad and F. Caballero. Extended criteria for organ acceptance: Strategies for achieving organ safety and for increasing organ pool. *Clin Transplant, Blackwell Munksgaard*, 17:308–324, 2003.

[7] A. Moreno, A. Valls, and J. Bocio. Management of hospital teams for organ transplants using multi-agent systems. In *AIME*, pages 374–383, 2001.

[8] ONT. Organización Nacional de Transplantes. http://www.ont.es.

[9] P.Tolchinsky, U. Corts, S. Modgil, F. Caballero, and A. Lpez-Navidad. Increasing human-organ transplant availability: Argumentation-based agent deliberation. *IEEE Intelligent Systems*, 21(6):30–37, 2006.

[10] P. Tolchinsky, S. Modgil, and U. Cortés. Argument schemes and critical questions for heterogeneous agents to argue over the viability of a human organ. In *AAAI 2006 Spring Symposium Series; Argumentation for Consumers of Healthcare*, 2006.

---

[6]http://www.lsi.upc.edu/~tolchinsky/ASR

[11] P. Tolchinsky, S. Modgil, U. Cortés, and M. Sànchez-Marrè. CBR and Argument Schemes for Collaborative Decision Making. In P. E. Dunne and T. J. M. Bench-Capon, editors, *Conference on Computational Models of Argument (COMMA 06)*, volume 144 of *Frontiers in Artificial Intelligence and Aplications*, pages 71–82. IOS Press, September 2006.

[12] J. Vázquez-Salceda, U. Cortés, J. Padget, A. López-Navidad, and F. Caballero. The organ allocation process: a natural extension of the CARREL Agent-Mediated Electronic Institution. *AiCommunications. The European Journal on Artificial Intelligence*, 3(16), 2003.

[13] D. N. Walton. *Argumentation Schemes for Presumptive Reasoning.* Lawrence Erlbaum Associates, Mahwah, NJ, USA, 1996.

Acknowledgment

This research was supported in part by EC Project ASPIC (FP6-IST-002307)

Pancho Tolchinsky and Ulises Cortés
Dept. Llenguatges i Sistemes informàtics
Universitat Politècnica de Catalunya
Jordi Girona 1-3
Barcelona 08034
Spain
e-mail: tolchinsky@lsi.upc.edu
        ia@lsi.upc.edu

Dan Grecu
Advanced Computation Lab, Cancer Research UK
e-mail: dan@grecu.net

Whitestein Series in Software Agent Technologies, 95–115

K4Care: Knowledge-Based Homecare e-Services for an Ageing Europe

Fabio Campana, Antonio Moreno, David Riaño and László Z. Varga

1. Introduction

Increasing longevity and increasing survival to acute accidents and diseases - in addition to the increase in the numbers of elderly people - imply an increased prevalence of chronic morbidity and disability. The elderly population needing full time care is considered as equivalent to the percentage of severely disabled elderly, which in turn is estimated to be 5% for the 65-69 year-old age group, 10% for the 70-79 age group, and 30% for the 80 and over age group [2]; this population can sum up to ten million people in the EU 25 area [3]. The care of chronic and disabled patients involves life long treatment under continuous expert supervision. Moreover, healthcare professionals and patients agree that institutionalization in hospitals or residential facilities may be unnecessary and even counterproductive. Home Care (HC) has been considered as a fundamental component of a network of long term care facilities, capable of reducing institutionalization, expenses and risk of death. The objective of an effective HC has the direct social implication of helping people partially or completely dependent to live in their environment as long as possible, and to contrast the improper use of institutionalization. It has to be considered that the care of the HC Patient (HCP) is particularly complex because of the growing number of people in such circumstances, because of the great amount of resources required to guarantee a quality long-term assistance, and because the typical HCP is an elderly patient, with co-morbid conditions and diseases, cognitive and/or physical impairment, functional loss from multiple disabilities, and impaired self-dependency.

All this complexity is captured in the K4CARE project (IST 2004-026968) [4], whose main objective was defined to be the combination of health care and ICT experiences coming from several western and eastern EU countries to create, implement, and validate a knowledge-based health care model for the professional assistance to senior patients at home. The first step of the project was to develop a health care K4CARE Model to guide the realization of an integrated system of

HC services supported by ICT technologies for the care of the elderly, the disabled persons, and the patients with chronic diseases in Europe. The interaction between health professionals, computer scientists, technology centres, and SMEs has been basic to define the model, providing detailed information about the structure of a Nuclear Service of HC and a prototype of Accessory Service (namely a Rehabilitation Unit) as an example of possible implementation of the structure. The K4CARE Model provides a paradigm easily adoptable in the EU Countries, being all the proposed structures filtered according to national laws.

The next section of this chapter describes the basic constituents of the K4CARE Model. The main ones are the *actors* (users of the system), the *actions* they may perform, the *services* provided by the system, and the *procedures* that implement those services. After that, the declarative and procedural knowledge used within the system is detailed. Declarative knowledge is represented in *ontologies*, whereas procedural knowledge is codified in a new formalism called *SDA**. Finally, the K4CARE agent-based system is presented. It has a *knowledge layer*, containing all the data needed by the system, a *data abstraction layer*, that provides transparent access to data, and the web-accessible agent-based *K4CARE platform*.

2. The K4CARE Model

K4CARE recommends a modular structure that can be adapted to different local opportunities and needs. As shown in figure 1, the K4CARE Model [5] is based on a nuclear structure (HCNS) which comprises the minimum number of common elements needed to provide a basic HC service. The HCNS can be extended with an optional number of Accessory Services (HCAS) that can be modularly added to the nuclear structure. These services will respond to specialized types of care, specific needs, opportunities, means, attending for example nutritional or oncology issues. The distinction between the HCNS and the complementary HCASs must be interpreted as a way of introducing flexibility and adaptability in the model. Each of the HC structures (i.e., HCNS and HCASs) consists of the same components: Actors, all the sort of human figures included in the structure of HC; Professional Actions and Liabilities, the actions that each actor performs to provide a service within the HC structure; Services, all the utilities provided by the HC structure for the care of the HCP; Procedures, the chain of events that leads an actor in performing actions to provide services; Information Documents, the documents required and produced by the actors to provide services in the HC structure.

2.1. Actors

In HC several persons interact: patients, relatives, physicians, social assistants, nurses, rehabilitation professionals, informal care givers, citizens, social organisms, etc. In the HCNS, these individuals have been considered as *actors* of the model. Apart from the patient which was defined above, actors are the Family Doctor (physician in charge of the patient), the Physician in Charge of the HC (medical

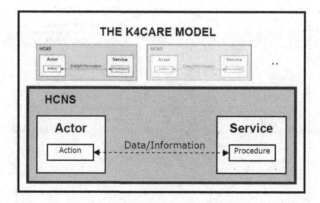

FIGURE 1. The *K4CARE* Model Architecture

responsible of the HC service, who in some countries or areas may correspond to the Family Doctor), the Head Nurse (who mainly coordinates the accomplishment of the intervention plan), the Social Worker (that identifies, evaluates, and deals with social needs), and the Nurse (provider of nursing care).

The *Evaluation Unit (EU)* is a temporary team aimed at the assessment and re-evaluations; the EU assesses the problems, defines the individual intervention plan, identifies the proper procedures, and evaluates the results. It is composed by the Family Doctor, the Physician in Charge of the HC, the Head Nurse, and the Social Worker. Other groups of professionals and non professional individuals are usually part of the HC. Their presence is almost ubiquitous, even if their position can hardly be comprised inside the core structure of HC. These groups of caregivers do not have an exact and definite position in the context of the HC network, but their role results, in most cases, fundamental for the continuous care of the HCP. For these reasons, they have been included in the K4CARE Model, and labelled as Additional Care Givers. Their individual presence in a particular HCNS is optional. They are: the Specialist Physician (medical doctor specialized in one branch of Medicine), the Social Operator (operative support to social needs), the Continuous Care Provider (person who is in charge of the continuous care of the HCP), and the Informal Care Giver (who provides support, without professional or familiar relationships).

The Actors have been considered to be members of three different groups: the patient, the stable members of HCNS (i.e., Family Doctor, Physician in Charge of HC, Head Nurse, Nurse, Social Worker), and the Additional Care Givers. Figure 2 shows the patient (i.e., the HCP) in the centre of the HCNS of the K4CARE Model, and the rest of the groups organised around him/her as a symbol of a patient-oriented HC model.

HCAS may introduce additional actors to support new services. For example, the Rehabilitation Unit or HCAS-R introduces the following actors into the HC system: Patient to rehabilitate (i.e., a person who suffers from the consequences of

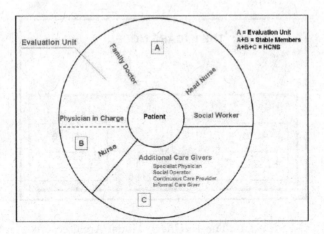

FIGURE 2. Actors of the HCNS

a condition which diminishes physical capability or from a functional impairment, such as immobility syndrome), Physician in Charge of the Rehabilitation Service, Therapists (as Physical Therapist, Occupational Therapist, or Speech and Language Therapist), Rehabilitation Service Coordinator (coordinates the work of the therapists), and Psychologist.

2.2. Professional Actions and Liabilities

Once the Actors are introduced, the Actions they perform in their duties for the model to provide Services have to be defined. These actions form the list of general actions that the actors are expected to perform with relation to their professional liabilities. So, HCNS Actions are the set of professional liabilities required to accomplish the procedures that implement the care services of the HCNS. The HCNS actions are grouped into: Patient Actions, Back Office Actions, Evaluation Unit Actions, Medical Actions, Medical Actions performed by the Family Doctor, Medical Actions performed by the Specialist Physician, Nursing Actions, Case Management Actions, and Social Actions. The number of Actions sums up to eighty-four (see [5]). Different combinations of sub-sets of those Actions individuate the different Services. In the HCAS - Rehabilitation Unit the Actions are: Patient Actions, Back Office Actions, Physician in Charge of the Rehabilitation Service Actions, Case Management Actions, and Rehabilitative Actions.

2.3. Services

The K4CARE Model provides a set of services for the care of HCP. In the HCNS these services are classified into Access Services, Patient Care Services, and Information Services. A complete list of this classification of HCNS services is reported in table 1.

    Access Services see the Actors of the HCNS as elements of the K4CARE model and they address issues like patient's admission and discharge from the HC

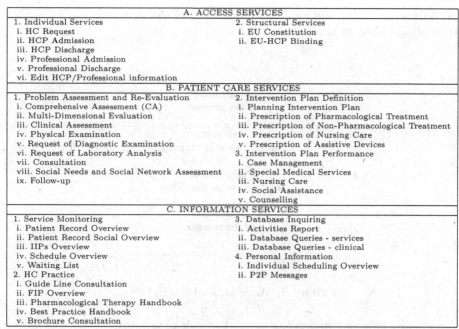

A. ACCESS SERVICES	
1. Individual Services	2. Structural Services
i. HC Request	i. EU Constitution
ii. HCP Admission	ii. EU-HCP Binding
iii. HCP Discharge	
iv. Professional Admission	
v. Professional Discharge	
vi. Edit HCP/Professional information	
B. PATIENT CARE SERVICES	
1. Problem Assessment and Re-Evaluation	2. Intervention Plan Definition
i. Comprehensive Assessment (CA)	i. Planning Intervention Plan
ii. Multi-Dimensional Evaluation	ii. Prescription of Pharmacological Treatment
iii. Clinical Assessment	iii. Prescription of Non-Pharmacological Treatment
iv. Physical Examination	iv. Prescription of Nursing Care
v. Request of Diagnostic Examination	v. Prescription of Assistive Devices
vi. Request of Laboratory Analysis	3. Intervention Plan Performance
vii. Consultation	i. Case Management
viii. Social Needs and Social Network Assessment	ii. Special Medical Services
ix. Follow-up	iii. Nursing Care
	iv. Social Assistance
	v. Counselling
C. INFORMATION SERVICES	
1. Service Monitoring	3. Database Inquiring
i. Patient Record Overview	i. Activities Report
ii. Patient Record Social Overview	ii. Database Queries - services
iii. IIPs Overview	iii. Database Queries - clinical
iv. Schedule Overview	4. Personal Information
v. Waiting List	i. Individual Scheduling Overview
2. HC Practice	ii. P2P Messages
i. Guide Line Consultation	
ii. FIP Overview	
iii. Pharmacological Therapy Handbook	
iv. Best Practice Handbook	
v. Brochure Consultation	

TABLE 1. Services of the HCNS

model. Access Services are oriented towards the organization of Actors and groups involved in the care of HCP: Individual Services allow actors to be related to the K4CARE Model and are used to admit, to discharge or to edit information about the people that is part of the model, whereas Structural Services are the HCNS Services to define the Evaluation Units in the K4CARE Model.

Patient Care Services are the most complex services of the model. HC is based upon the synergic actions of the actors, including the assessment of the problem and the identification of the needs of the HCP, the definition of an Individual Intervention Plan (IIP), its accomplishment through the proper procedures, and the evaluation of the results. This step-by-step process can be executed several times, until the achievement of proper results. This work cycle of the HCNS is summarized in figure 3. Following this sequence, Patient Care Services are classified into Problem Assessment, Intervention Plan Definition, and Intervention Plan Performance. All the HCNS services for assessing the problem aim at diagnosing the patient situation and re-evaluating over time the results of the intervention. The services to define the intervention plan aim at choosing the most promising course of actions (i.e., treatment) based on the individualization of best practice. The services to perform the IIP are those addressed by the application of a general intervention plan to a concrete HCP. This Individual Intervention Plan includes and defines the means and modalities aimed at evaluating results and measuring the implications of its application.

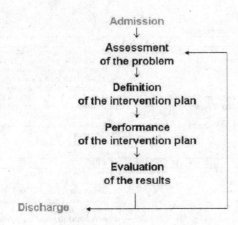

FIGURE 3. Work cycle of the HCNS

Finally, *Information Services* cover the needs of information that the HCNS actors require in the model. Information Services allow access to the information and the knowledge that the system contains. Such services are provided to any HC actor, without relation to a particular Care Service. The provided nformation and knowledge can be used for different purposes, mainly service monitoring, social issues, clinical issues, and health care related topics.

2.4. Procedures

When the actors, the actions they perform inside the model, and the services of the model have been established, it has to be defined the way these actions are performed by the actors and merged to provide specific services. In the K4CARE Model a procedure represents the way that the actions provided by/to the actors are combined to accomplish one service. Procedures for each of the services have been defined, indicating the sequence (or possibly alternative sequences) of actions to be followed in order to provide the service. For each action, the procedures indicate the actors who are requested/liable of performing that particular action. In this way, a service is defined by the set of actions needed and by the actors requested/liable to perform them.

    The definition of the procedures has been realized both for the HCNS and the HCAS - Rehabilitation Unit.

2.5. Information Documents

The K4CARE Model defines a set of information units whose main purpose is to provide information about the care processes realized by the Actors to accomplish a Service. Different kinds of Actors will be supplied with specific information that will help them to carry out their duties in the K4CARE Model. All these data are considered to be part of Documents. Documents will constitute the basis for the realization of the Electronic Home Care Record, specifically realized for the project.

Different sets of Documents have been defined for each group of Services. For each Document the right of access for each Actor has been defined, as to say, it has been indicated which Actor(s) is liable to read and/or to write a specific Document. The Actors involved in the different Patient Care Services and Procedures can contribute to the generation of the Document (write option) or may require the total or partial information the Document hosts (read option). The interaction between Actors and Documents is then defined by the options read (R), write (W) or both (RW).

Regarding Documents supporting the actors taking part in the Patient Care Services, it seemed sensible to define the information they contain approaching as much as possible the usual health care practice. Since these Documents may have different general purposes inside the different sets of Services and Procedures, they have been sub-divided into Request Documents, Authorization Documents, Prescription Documents, and Anamnestic Documents. Request Documents contain information about a request of a Service, an Action of a Service, an appointment; they usually initiate a Procedure for a Service or a part of it. Authorization Documents are used to confirm and to authorize a certain Action to be performed; they are connected with key points in the development of a Procedure. Prescription Documents contain the instructions deriving from a medical action. Anamnestic Documents contain information about the patient that will be historically used in the process of care. The same principles guided the definition of the Documents both for the HCNS and the HCAS - Rehabilitation Unit.

Information Service Documents report on underlying activities - even analyzed through semi-automatic queries - or on officially recognized information, related to HC. A special Service is represented by the possibility of exchanging messages among Actors.

2.6. MultiDimensional Evaluation

Inside the K4CARE Model, special attention has been devoted to the definition of a set of evaluation scales to be used for the assessment of the HCP. Since the main methodological issue in the model is represented by the multi-dimensional approach – applying to any of the sub-structures of the model (evaluation, intervention, and staff) – Comprehensive Geriatric Assessment served as model for the process of assessment, the MultiDimensional Evaluation (MDE). MDE differs from a standard medical evaluation by including non-medical domains, by emphasizing functional ability and quality of life, and by relying on interdisciplinary teams [6-16] This assessment aids in the diagnosis of health-related problems, development of plans for treatment and follow-up, coordination of care, determination of the need for long-term care, and optimal use of health care resources. MDE in the K4CARE Model is based on a set of standardized evaluation scales largely accepted and used by international teams for clinical care and research purposes. MDE has been organised in a two-level structure: first level, to be performed for all the HCPs; second level, to be performed in presence of immobility syndrome or cognitive impairment (figure 4).

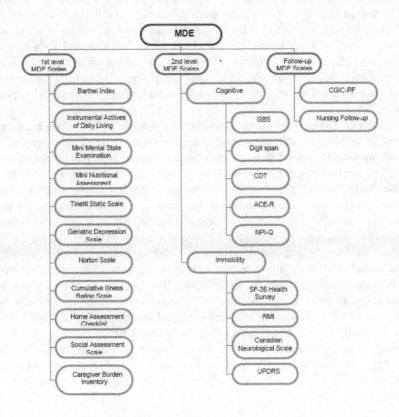

FIGURE 4. MultiDimensional Evaluation

3. Domain knowledge

The implementation of the *K4CARE* Model is sustained on the formal representation of home care knowledge. A distinction is made between declarative knowledge and procedural knowledge. On one hand, declarative knowledge comprises both all the statements representing the principles of the HC model, and the health care and medical background which is required in the treatment of patients at home. On the other hand, procedural knowledge in K4CARE represents the way in which home care must be provided.

In the next subsections two ontologies and the SDA* knowledge representation model are introduced. These three elements define the Knowledge level of the K4CARE project.

3.1. The Actor Profile Ontology

The *Actor Profile Ontology (APO)* gathers all the knowledge about the profiles of the subjects involved in the K4CARE model: health care professionals, patients and relatives, citizens, and social organisms. This knowledge is employed to customize the interaction of K4CARE with these subjects. The APO is defined as the interrelation of several families of concepts. The main concepts in the APO are Entity, Service, Action, Procedure, Document, SDA, and Care Unit Element.

- An entity is defined as an actor (person or group) that K4CARE is able to interact with,
- a service is each one of the services the K4CARE Model provides (see section 2.3),
- an action is an indivisible activity that an entity is able to perform within the model,
- a procedure is the way in which a service is implemented,
- a SDA is a combination of actions in order to provide a formal representation of a procedure, and
- a care unit element is either the HCNS or one of the HCAS that are included in the K4CARE model.

Each one of the above concepts is the root of a hierarchy (or family) of subconcepts that are connected by means of class-subclass relationships. So, for example, in figure 5 a *Nurse* is a *Stable Member* of the HCNS, a *Stable Member* is an *Actor* (i.e., person), and an *Actor* is an *Entity*.

The *hierarchy of entities* distinguishes between *actors* which are individual persons, and *groups* which are teams that work as a single unit. An actor can be either a *patient* or an *additional care giver* or a *stable member* (recall figure 2). Whenever a new entity is introduced by the incorporation of a new HCAS to the K4CARE Model, this entity is introduced as a subclass in the hierarchy. For example, when the HCAS-R (i.e., Rehabilitation Unit) is introduced, the concept *Patient to Rehabilitate* is incorporated as subclass of *Patient*, the actor *Physician in Charge of the Rehabilitation Service* as subclass of *Physician in Charge*, and *Physical Therapist* as subclass of a new subclass *Therapist* which is subclass of *Additional Care Giver*.

Similar hierarchies are established for services and actions following the indications of the K4CARE Model that are reported in sections 2.3 and 2.2, and also for the rest of root concepts [17] (i.e., procedure, document, SDA, and care unit element).

The APO is extended with a set of properties that permit the definition of relationships among the above mentioned concepts. The most relevant properties are *hasMember* that indicates which are the actors integrating a concrete group

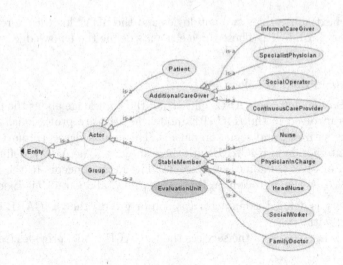

FIGURE 5. The Hierarchy of Entities for HCNS

(e.g., in the HCNS, the *Evaluation Unit* is defined to "hasMember" Family Doctor, Physician in Charge of HC, Head Nurse, and Social Worker); *doesAction* that permits the introduction of restrictions on whether an entity is allowed to perform an action or not; *initiatesService* to restrict which entity may or may not start a service; *isStepOf* which indicates an action is part of a procedure; *hasProcedure* to relate one service to its possible procedures, or *readsDocument* and *writesDocument* to indicate which actors are able to read or write a document while performing a concrete action. A detailed explanation of all the APO properties can be found in [17].

3.2. The Case Profile Ontology

The *Case Profile Ontology (CPO)* is a complex structure that aims at capturing and representing in a formal way all the health care knowledge required for the treatment of Home Care Patients in K4CARE. So far, the APO has been designed to integrate concepts related to the syndromes of cognitive impairment and immobility. The main concepts in the CPO are Syndrome, Disease, Signs and Symptoms, Social Issues, Problem Assessment, and Intervention.

- a *syndrome* is a complex health situation in which a combination of signs and symptoms occurs more frequently than would be expected on the basis of chance alone,
- a *disease* is a physiological or psychological dysfunction in the *International Classification of Diseases, Injuries, and Causes of Death 10th revision (ICD10)*,
- a *social issue* is a patient environment characteristic that modifies the patient condition and needs social intervention,

- a *social assessment* is an objective criterion to evaluate a sign or a symptom, and
- an *intervention* is a measure that is taken to deal with a patient condition.

All these concepts are the roots of their respective hierarchies in which each concept can be related to several subconcepts by means of class-subclass relationships. For example, in the hierarchy of diseases depicted in figure 6, *Alzheimer* is defined as a subclass of *Dementia*, which is a *Disease*.

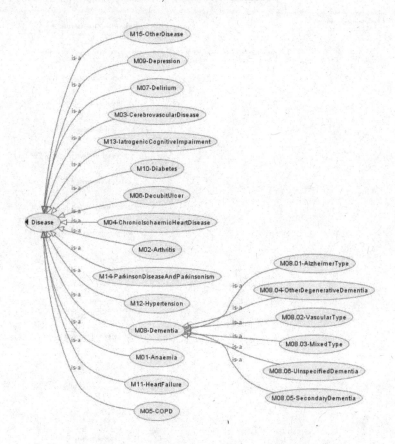

FIGURE 6. The Hierarchy of general Diseases

The *hierarchy of Problem Assessment* is provided in figure 7 as a sample of the extension of the CPO. The remaining hierarchies are published in [17].

The CPO incorporates several properties to define restrictions on the relationships among concepts (see figure 8). The most relevant properties are: *hasIntervention* that relates a social issue, a syndrome or a disease with an intervention, *isSignOf* that relates a social issue, a syndrome or a disease with its signs and symptoms, *evaluates* that connects a problem assessment with the signs and symptoms

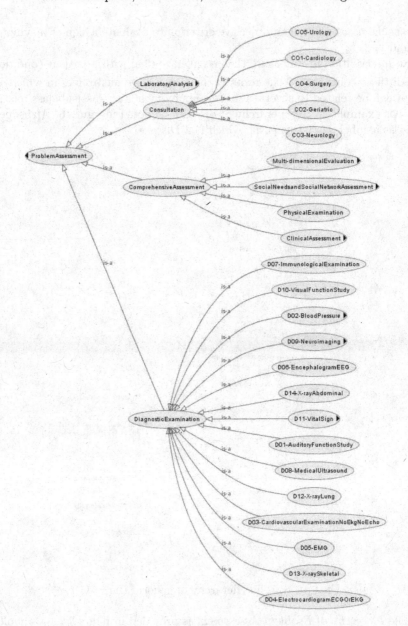

FIGURE 7. The Hierarchy of Problem Assessment

it assesses, and *canBeCauseOf* that indicates what are the diseases that can cause a syndrome.

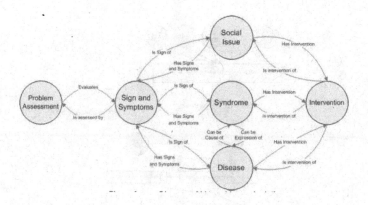

FIGURE 8. CPO Properties as Relationships

3.3. The SDA* Model

The SDA* Model is an effective framework to formalize procedural knowledge (i.e., procedures, FIPs, and IIPs) in the K4CARE project. The SDA* model is based on the concept of *flowchart* but it is extended with several elements to ease the representation of procedural knowledge in health care, as for example, the concept of state as starting point that allows the execution of the chart from different points, or the introduction of time constraints to introduce time restrictions in medical procedures.

The SDA* Model is based on a set of terms that can be divided into state terms, decision terms, and action terms. *State terms* define the vocabulary that is used to describe the feasible patient conditions or situations in the area of interest (e.g., terms as high-blood-pressure to establish a differential treatment or insured-patient to define the coverage of the patient). *Decision terms* are the terminology that health care professionals use to condition the sort of treatment to be followed (e.g., terms as female or antecedents-of-heart-problems that derive the course of professional activities in one or another direction). *Action terms* are the way that medical, surgical, clinical or management activities are identified (e.g., terms as take-beta-blocker, avoid-salt-in-meals, make-blood-analysis, or visit-endocrinologist are respective examples of prescription, counseling, ordering a test, or consulting a specialist, which are types of medical actions that may appear in the description of a treatment).

A subset of the set of state terms define a patient *state*, while subsets of action terms describe *actions*. States represent patient conditions, situations, or statuses that deserve a particular course of action which is totally or partially different from the actions followed when the patient is in other state. Actions constitute the proper health care activity in the SDA* Model. *Decisions* act as join elements between states and actions and they allow the integration of the variability of a treatment in terms of the available information about the patient. Finally, states,

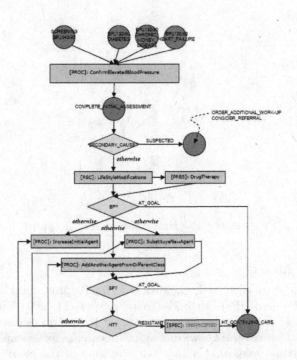

FIGURE 9. SDA* representing a FIP to diagnose hypertension

decisions, and actions which are respectively represented as circles, rhombuses, and squares, are connected to represent procedural knowledge in medicine [18] as figure 9 depicts.

In the K4CARE project, the SDA* representation model is used to codify the procedures introduced in section 2.4, Formal Intervention Plans (FIP) as sound descriptions of evidence-based health care interventions, and Individual Intervention Plans (IIP) as costumizations of a FIP to a concrete patient.

4. The K4CARE system

The basic technical target of the K4CARE project is the design and implementation of an agent-based web-accessible platform that provides to the system users the services defined in the *K4CARE model*. This section describes the three-layered architecture in which the *K4CARE platform* is embedded, and it explains how the agents in the multi-agent system coordinate their activities to support health care professionals to provide home care services.

4.1. The K4CARE architecture

The architecture of the K4CARE system is divided in three main modules: the *Knowledge Layer*, the *Data Abstraction Layer*, and the *K4CARE agent-based platform* (see figure 10).

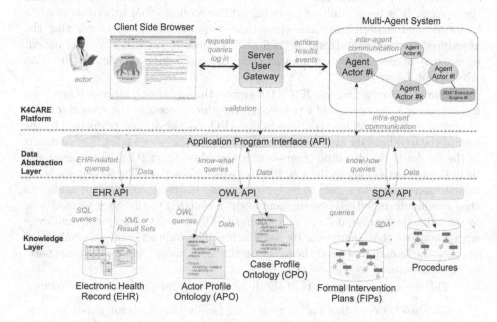

FIGURE 10. *K4CARE* architecture

The *Knowledge Layer* includes all the data sources required by the platform, described in section 3. It contains an *Electronic Health Care Record* (EHCR) that stores patient records (i.e., personal information, examination results, treatments). The EHCR also contains the *Individual Intervention Plan (IIP)* that has to be applied to the patient. The declarative -organisational and medical- knowledge (know-what) is represented in the APO and CPO ontologies, using OWL. Medical *procedures* (that describe the steps to be taken to deliver a *service*, as explained in section 2) are coded using the SDA* representation formalism described in the previous section and stored in a repository. *Formal Intervention plans* (FIPs), which are descriptions, provided by health care organisations, of the way in which a specific disease, syndrome or symptom should be treated, are also represented using the SDA* language and stored in a concrete database.

The *Data Abstraction Layer* provides some Java-based methods that allow the *K4Care* platform entities to retrieve the data and knowledge they need to perform their tasks. That layer offers a wide set of high level queries that provide transparency between the data (knowledge) and its use (platform) [1].

4.2. The K4CARE platform

The upper layer, the *K4CARE platform*, is a web-based application with a client side and a server side. The home care services are provided by a set of permanent agents (*Agent Actors* in figure 10). There is one permanent agent for each of the users of the system. This agent represents the corresponding actor within the system. It is responsible of receiving all the requests that other actors make to its associated user, communicating these requests to the user, receiving the appropriate responses and sending them to the requesting actors. These permanent agents may access the system knowledge by using the API provided by the Data Abstraction Layer [1].

Human actors access the *K4CARE system* through a web browser. Once they log in (giving a username and a password), they have access to the system services according to their profile restrictions in the APO. All the actions performed by the user in the web browser are received by a servlet (in the server side). The first task of the servlet is the dynamic creation of a *Gateway Agent* (GA). This agent will be in the system as long as the web browser session is active. The servlet sends the information related to a user to its corresponding Gateway Agent. This agent can then communicate with the permanent agent associated to that user to receive or to send the appropriate data at each moment. Thus, each GA only communicates with the agent that represents its same actor. The bidirectional communication between the human users and the agents in the MAS always follows the same path: $user_i \leftrightarrow$ browser $\leftrightarrow$ servlet $\leftrightarrow GA_i \leftrightarrow agent_i$.

The two basic components of the *K4CARE web interface* are the following:

- Each user, depending on its type (i.e., family doctor, head nurse, patient, etc.) may request a set of services from the platform (e.g., a family doctor may request the comprehensive assessment of a patient, or a social worker may request the social network assessment of a patient). The web interface provides a tree-like view of the services available to each user. Before requesting a service, the user has to identify the patient on which the service will be applied.

- When a service is requested, a workflow-like *procedure* will be executed. Procedures include the performance of different actions, possibly related to different kinds of actors. For example, when a comprehensive assessment is requested, different steps (concerning family doctors, the physician in charge of the HC unit, social workers and the head nurse) have to be taken. Thus, different *Actor Agents* will receive requests to perform specific actions. When a user starts the browser session, he/she will see in the web interface an area with a list of all the pending actions that have been requested to that user (those actions will have been sent from the user's permanent agent to the browser, via the user's Gateway Agent and the servlet). If the user selects one action of the list, the web interface will display the *document* to be filled after having made that action. When the document is filled, it will be sent to the corresponding permanent agent (via the servlet and the user Gateway

Agent), who will tell the requesting agent that the action it had requested has been done. The document will be stored in the EHCR of the patient to keep track of the medical activities that have been made on the user.

When a patient enters the system, his/her physical, clinical and social states are assessed by an *Evaluation Unit* (EU), composed by the physician in charge of the Home Care unit, a family doctor, the head nurse and a social worker. The results of the comprehensive assessment are carefully analysed and the diseases, signs and symptoms of the patient are identified. After that, the platform retrieves the FIPs associated to each of them. This set of FIPs is merged, to get a single Formal Intervention Plan that takes into account all the problems of the patient. Finally, this FIP is turned by the EU into an *Individual Intervention Plan* (IIP) by tailoring it to the specific personal circumstances of the patient. After that, the intelligent agents in the K4CARE platform, as will be seen in the next section, have to coordinate their activities to execute the different steps of the IIP to provide the care to the patient. It is worth noting that both IIPs and procedures are represented in the SDA* formalism; thus, the tasks that the agents have to carry out to execute a procedure (when a user requests from the platform a particular service) are exactly the same than those they have to make to enact an Individual Intervention Plan.

4.3. The K4CARE Service execution

The K4CARE platform will provide services to its users like patients, family doctors, physicians in charge, nurses, head nurses, social workers, etc. Each user will achieve its goals with the help of a set of services specific to his or her user type. A set of services specific to a user type will be incorporated in an agent. The agents may be distributed in the computer network. The services will invoke other services and thus the K4Care platform will have a distributed service-oriented architecture. Some of the services will correspond to medical processes (see table 1) and their execution procedures will be based on medical guidelines (i.e., evidence-based medicine), while other services will correspond to administrative or technical procedures related to the operation of the platform or the home care centre.

The K4CARE service model is derived from the processes of home care and it is based on the following concepts:

- *Service*: in section 2.3, services in the K4CARE Model were defined as complex activities which are typically accomplished in collaboration with several actors (see also task below). A service is identified by a unique name (or service id) and it may have several instantiations which are called *procedures*. Different procedures instantiating the same service may be for example different localisations of the same service, e.g., in different countries or medical centres. However, in a given K4CARE platform installation, each service has one and only one procedure instantiation.
- *Procedure*: derived from the K4CARE Model, a procedure in the K4CARE system is a formal description of a set of *tasks* organized in some workflow

(sequential, parallel, preconditions, etc.). The procedure may be the instantiation of a medical or any general process in the medical centre. If the procedure is the instantiation of a medical process, then we call it *Intervention Plan* (IP). The workflow control structures of the procedure are described in the SDA* formal medical guideline language similar to Proforma [20, 21] or Asbru [22]. Tasks can invoke the services of another agent in the system, therefore a procedure may be some composition of services. The execution of a service is started by retrieving its procedure from the local system, and then the procedure is executed in an interpreted way step-by-step. All the services available in the given K4CARE installation are registered by pairs (*ServiceName*, *Procedure*) at system start. Procedures and IPs are created by humans, e.g., medical centre managers or physicians.

- *Task*: it is an execution step in a procedure and it is usually a request to execute another service. The task is described by an n-tuple: task = (subject, object, service or action, doc). The *subject* is the agent which is expected to execute the *service* or the *action*. For example, the agent of a specific nurse or the physician in charge. The *object* is the actor on which the service is expected to be executed (e.g., a specific patient). The *doc* is a document relating to the *service*. All actors are expected to document their activities in this document. There may be other optional parameters. It might be possible that the subject corresponds to the same agent that executes the current procedure. In this case the service is executed internally.

- *Action*: it is any activity that can be executed by the agent on its own, i.e., requires no invocation of the service of another agent. The set of actions that an agent can perform can be considered as the agent skills and it is part of the knowledge in the Agent Profile Ontology (APO). Each action of the agent is provided as a service for the system for other agents. When an action is executed, no procedure description retrieval is needed. Actions have unique names and can be imagined as a piece of Java code that implements the action.

Figure 11 shows the relation of services, procedures and tasks. Service S1 has two procedure instantiations: P1.1 and P1.2, but in this system only P1.1 is installed. For a given patient Oy, the first task of P1.1 invokes service S2 which is provided by the agent Bx and that has P2.1 as installed procedure. After the execution of P2.1 is completed (see dashed square on the right of the figure), the control returns to P1.1 where the next task contains an action A1 which is executed locally.

The diagram also shows the possibility of the K4CARE system to execute parallel and conditional tasks.

4.4. The K4Care Platform and EHCR Systems

In the process of supporting the home care activities by providing home care services as described above, the K4Care platform must have to retrieve data from the EHCR system as well, because the medical data of the patient from previous

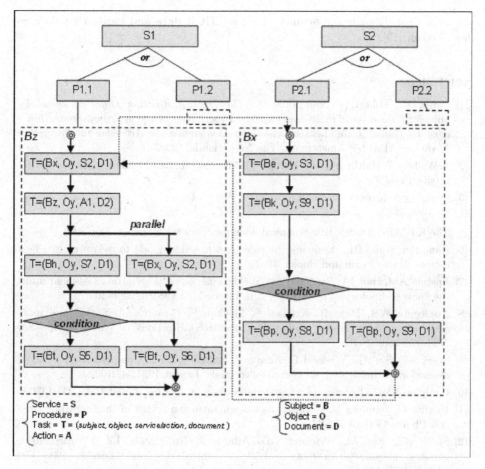

FIGURE 11. An example of the service model of the K4Care informatics environment

treatment may be necessary for the current home care activity. The needed data might have been produced in a former treatment or a most recent treatment. If the data was produced in a most recent treatment, for example just after the patient was released from the hospital to his or her home, and the home care centre is in interaction with the institute where the data was produced, then the needed data can be easily located and retrieved through EHCR data exchange standards, because the location and the reference of the data is known. However if the data was produced in a former treatment, for example years ago in a hospital, when home care was not envisaged for the patient, then locating the data is difficult, because there is no direct interaction between the hospital and the home care centre. In this case the physician does not know and even the patient might not remember that there is some relevant data in that hospital. This is when provenance awareness can help to realise the importance of some EHCR data and locate that data as described in [19].

References

[1] Batet, M., Gibert, K. and Valls, A. *The Data Abstraction Layer as knowledge provider for a medical multi-agent system*. Proceedings of the workshop *From Knowledge to Global Care*, held at the *11th Conference on Artificial Intelligence in Medicine*, AIME07. Amsterdam, The Netherlands, (2007).

[2] A Walker, T Maltby. Ageing Europe - 1997 - Buckingham; Philadelphia: Open University Press

[3] http://epp.eurostat.cec.eu.int/portal/

[4] http://www.k4care.net/

[5] The K4CARE Model. D01 technical document, www.k4care.net, Dec 2006.

[6] Kane RA, Kane RL. Assessing the elderly: a practical guide to measurement. Lexington, Mass.: Lexington Books, 1981.

[7] Epstein AM, Hall JA, Besdine R, et al. The emergence of geriatric assessment units: the "new technology of geriatrics." Ann Intern Med 1987;106:299-303.

[8] Applegate WB, Deyo R, Kramer A, Meehan S. Geriatric evaluation and management: current status and future research directions. J Am Geriatr Soc 1991;39:Suppl:2S-7S.

[9] Stuck AE, Siu AL, Wieland D, Adams J, Rubenstein LZ. Comprehensive geriatric assessment: a meta-analysis of controlled trials. Lancet 1993;342:1032-6.

[10] Campion EW. The value of geriatric interventions. N Engl J Med 1995; 332:1376-8.

[11] Unguru G, Feinberg M. Geriatric assessment teams: a review of the literature. Consult Pharm 1998;13:553-63

[12] Stuck AE, Siu AL, Wieland GD, Adams J, Rubenstein LZ. Comprehensive geriatric assessment: a meta-analysis of controlled trials". Lancet. 1993 Oct 23;342(8878):1032-6.

[13] Nikolaus T, Specht-Leible N, Bach M, Oster P and Schlierf G. A randomized trial of comprehensive geriatric assessment and home intervention in the care of hospitalized patients. Age and Ageing,1999; Vol 28, 543-550

[14] Fretwell MD, Raymond PM, McGarvey ST et al. The senior Care Study: a controlled trial of consultative/unit based geriatric assessment programme in acute care. J Am Geriatr Soc 1990;38:1973-81

[15] Landefeld CS, Palmer RM, Kresevic DM et al. A randomized trial of care in a hospital medical unit especially designed to improve the functional outcomes of acutely ill older patients. N Engl J Med 1995; 332:1338-44)

[16] Geriatric Interdisciplinary Teams in The Merck Manual of Geriatrics. Ed: Mark H. Beers, MD Copyright 2000-2006 by Merck & Co. 2005. Chapter 7.

[17] Riaño D., Casals J., Real F. The K4CARE Ontologies. Research Report, DEIM, URV, 2007.

[18] Riaño D. The SDA* Model: A Set Theory Approach. CBMS 2007, Maribor, Slovenia, (2007).

[19] Tamás Kifor, László Z. Varga, Javier Vázquez-Salceda, Sergio Álvarez, Steven Willmott, Simon Miles, Luc Moreau, *Provenance in Agent-Mediated Healthcare Systems*, IEEE Intelligent Systems, vol. 21, no. 6, pp. 38-46, Nov/Dec, 2006.

[20] Jonathan Bury, John Fox, David Sutton, *The PROforma guideline specification language: progress and prospects*, Proceedings of the First European Workshop, Computer-based Support for Clinical Guidelines and Protocols (EWGLP 2000), Leipzig 13-14 Nov. 2000.

[21] John Fox, Nicky Johns, Ali Rahmanzadeh, *Disseminating Medical Knowledge: the PROforma Approach*, Artificial Intelligence in Medicine, vol. 14, no. 1-2, pp. 157-182, 1998.

[22] Robert Kosara, Silvia Miksch, *Metaphors of Movement: A Visualization and User Interface for Time-Oriented, Skeletal Plans*, Artificial Intelligence in Medicine, vol. 22, no. 2, pp. 111-131, 2001.

Acknowledgment

The authors would like to acknowledge the support of the *K4Care* European project (IST 2004-026968): *Knowledge-based homecare e-services for an ageing Europe*. The following people have actively participated in the work described in this chapter:

- University Rovira i Virgili (URV, Tarragona): Montserrat Batet, Joan Casals, David Isern, Joan Albert López-Vallverdú, José Miguel Millán, Francis Real, and Albert Solé.
- University of Perugia: Sara Ercolani, and Patrizia Mecocci.
- Fondazione Santa Lucia: Carlo Caltagirone, and Roberta Annicchiarico.
- Computer and Automation Research Institute of the Hungarian Academy of Sciences (MTA SZTAKI): Gianfranco Pedone, Viktor Kelemen, and Tamás Kifor.

Fabio Campana
CAD
Lazio, Rome
e-mail: fcampana@tiscali.it

Antonio Moreno and David Riaño
Universitat Rovira i Virgili
Spain
e-mail: antonio.moreno@urv.cat
      david.riano@urv.cat

László Z. Varga
Computer and Automation Research Institute
Kende u. 13-17
1111 Budapest
Hungary
e-mail: laszlo.varga@sztaki.hu

Whitestein Series in Software Agent Technologies, 117–140
© 2007 Birkhäuser Verlag Basel/Switzerland

Supported Human Autonomy for Recovery and Enhancement of Cognitive and Motor Abilities Using Agent Technologies

Ulises Cortés, Roberta Annicchiarico, Cristina Urdiales, Cristian Barrué, Antonio Martínez, Alfredo Villar and Carlo Caltagirone

Abstract. The goal of *SHARE-it*, an EU FP6 funded project, is to develop a scalable, adaptive system of add-ons to sensor and assistive technology so that they can be modularly integrated into an intelligent home environment to enhance the individuals autonomy. The system will be designed to inform and assist the user and his/her caregivers through monitoring and mobility help. Thus, we plan to contribute to the development of the next generation of assistive devices for older persons or people with disabilities so that they can be self-dependent as long as possible. We focus on add-ons to be compatible with existing technologies and to achieve an easier integration into existing systems. We also aim at adaptive systems as transparent and, consequently, as easy to use to the person as possible. Scalability is meant to include or remove devices from the system in a simple, intuitive way. *SHARE-it* will provide an Agent-based Intelligent Decision Support System to aid the elders.

Keywords. Assistive Technologies, Agents.

1. Introduction

As Man [18] suggested, health is defined as "*not merely the absence of disease and infirmity*", but as "*a resource, which enables individuals to fulfil human potentials and maximize capabilities, achieve successes at work, enable social participation and enjoy a good Quality of Life*" (QoL). Accepting the position of viewing health

Authors would like to acknowledge the support of IRCCS Santa Lucia Ethical Committee for authorizing this experiment and to the individual participants. Authors would like to acknowledge support from the *SHARE-it*: Supported Human Autonomy for Recovery and Enhancement of cognitive and motor abilities using information technologies (FP6-IST-045088). The views expressed in this paper are not necessarily those of *SHARE-it* consortium.

as an integral part of life and well-being and the pursuit of health as a necessary and continuous lifelong process, it is the intent of this explorative idea address the health service needs and QoL of senior citizens and individuals with disabilities who live at home.

Since its very first inception computer-aided tools for healthcare have been designed to give support, in the first place, to caregivers in the decision-making and large efforts have been devoted to this aim. A change in this trend came along with the introduction of Assistive Technology (AT) to provide supportive and adaptive services to individuals who require assistance due to suffer some disabilities with the tasks of daily life this implies [22].

It is a well-known fact that the older adult population in the world is rapidly growing and is starting to demand greater access to improved healthcare and Assistive Technologies (AT) in order to improve quality of life (QoL). AT is a generic term that includes assistive, adaptive, and rehabilitative devices and the process used in selecting, locating, and using them. AT are designed to promote greater independence for people with physical and/or cognitive disabilities by enabling them to perform tasks that they were formerly unable to accomplish, or had great difficulty accomplishing, by providing enhancements to or changed methods of interacting with the technology needed to accomplish such tasks. According to Pollack, [23], AT can assist older people with mild cognitive impairment in one or more of the following ways:

1. by providing assurance that the elder is safe and is performing necessary daily activities, and, if not, alerting a caregiver;
2. by helping the elder compensate for her impairment, assisting in the performance of daily activities; and
3. by assessing the elders cognitive status.

The development and use of such technologies has started to become even more important as a growing proportion of this population has to deal with additional impairments beyond those related to the normal aging process, such as cognitive impairments (e.g., dementia or Alzheimers disease), sensory impairments (e.g., low vision and visual field reduction), or other motor and coordination conditions (e.g., spasticity and tremor) as explained in [20]. AT are becoming ubiquitous and many solutions are Agent-based[1].

New generations of technologies promise radical advances in ICT support for European elderly citizens with disabilities. Assistive engineering and design is a field at the intersection between technology, the natural sciences, the humanities, the social sciences, and medicine. AT are of special interest, as the average age of the population increases fast [6, 23]. Clearly, societal resources will not be sufficient

---

[1]An Agent is a goal-directed, computational entity which acts on behalf of another entity (or entities). Agent systems are self-contained software programs possessing domain knowledge and an ability to behave with some degree of independence to carry out actions to achieve specified goals. They are designed to operate in dynamically changing or unstable environments.

to assist all elderly or people with disabilities, so IST are expected to play a key role in this respect.

The power of AT is still under-recognised by physicians and its potential as an aid to patients is under-exploited. These technologies could be seen as a therapy or as a commodity. There are limits to the extent to which rehabilitation professionals can help to improve the skills of impaired people and the broader environments in which they live, and AT provide powerful means to overcome those limitations.

Despite technical advances however, design development and management of such systems still presents huge challenges. Experience with new technology has shown that increased computerization does not guarantee improved human-machine system performance. Poor use of technology can result in systems that are difficult to learn or use and even may lead to catastrophic errors (Norman, 1983). This may occur because, while there are typically reductions in physical workload, mental workload has increased (Weiner, 1989). This strong reliance on the user skills is a typical design failure. Interaction should be as natural as possible to avoid learning load. Cognitive research provides insight and guidance in areas such as the effects of practice on performance, rational decision-making, and expert problem-solving in the user interface.

This project addresses the fact that, in order to overcome the Digital Divide, technology must be adapted to the individual rather than the other way round: this need is particularly obvious where people with disabilities are concerned. Older persons and people with disabilities are not able to compensate for the deficiencies of the technology (the way other people often can) and thereby achieve a functioning system despite the lack of functionality. In other words, the interaction between the technology and disabled citizens makes it necessary to tackle the design of technical devices so that they will be usable by everyone and address the issue of shared autonomy. Services targeted at disabled people should aim at solving the problems, which also set open and promising lines of research in the following areas: physical aids, cognitive aids, patient monitoring, decision-making and human factors.

The main goal of the *SHARE-it* project is to contribute to the development of the next generation of intelligent and semi-autonomous assistive devices for older persons and people with disabilities (both cognitive and/or motorial) so that they can be self-dependent enough to autonomously live in the community, staying at home as long as possible with a maximum safety and comfort; this possibility would increase their quality of life, and, at the same time, delay their institutionalization.

With this context in mind, we introduced in [9] the design of an integrated architecture aimed at helping citizens with disabilities to improve their autonomy in structured, dynamic environments. The main element of this architecture is an intelligent agent layer that mediates between different technology components (robotic devices, ubiquitous computing, and interfaces) in order to provide the subject with the necessary degree of independent mobility to benefit from different assistive services and to reach goals determined by either the subject himself/herself or by medical staff.

The agent based control system provides an excellent means to model the different required autonomous elements in the patient's environment (from control elements in the wheelchair to care-giving services). Agents probe to be efficient in coordinating heterogeneous domain-specific elements with different levels of autonomy. Addressing the mobility problem and keeping in mind that different users need different degrees of help, a part of this agent based control layer has been focused on the development of a shared control for the robotic wheelchair that adapts to the user needs.

1.1. Plan of the chapter

From the previous section it becomes clear *how* critical it is for society to be able to deploy Safe and Sound AT devices. This chapter is organized as follows, in Section 2 we introduce our concept of Shared Autonomy and we position this concept in the field of AT. In Section 3 we explain an experimental set that we used to learn about the feasibility of using an Agent-based AT architecture embedded in an Intelligent Ambiance that we designed and discussed in [9] .

In Section 4 we present *SHARE-it*'s actual vision and we deeply discuss some of the issues that we think are key to provide a full and robust Agent-based solution.

In Section 5 we draw our conclusions on the use of the AI technologies to support and enhance the QoL of our target population and future work.

2. Shared Autonomy: A vision

Autonomy for the elderly or people with disabilities does not only rely on mobility terms, but on a set of domains influenced by functioning, activity limitations, participation restrictions and environmental factors. Life areas related to activities and participation are such as learning and applying knowledge, general tasks and demands, communication, mobility, self-care, interpersonal interactions and relationships as well as community and social life. All these domains can be affected by aging or disabilities and are the base of personal autonomy and the satisfactory participation on them reflects on the self well-being. AT can participate in these activities in order to enhance the user's autonomy, gathering all the environmental information and making use of it properly.

Our idea is based on the notion of a *Shared Autonomy* between the user and its own agent-based mediator with any information system at hand. Existing telematic healthcare systems that provide integrated services to users are not, to our taste, enough flexible to allow a real personalization and maybe now it is too expensive to change them.

The shared autonomy concept is scarcely explored in literature and often it is misunderstood as shared control (e.g., [29, 16]). In the personal autonomy and disability context, two different scenarios of the shared autonomy can be elicitaded.

- People presenting mainly physical impairments are able to define their own goals, but due to their restrictions they usually are not able to execute them, suffering a limitation in their autonomy. In this scenario the contribution of AT focus on physical devices, mostly mobility hardware, that allow them to reach their objectives. These devices may be controlled by multi-agent systems or through an agent supervised shared control if the user motor capabilities are not severely damaged. In this scenario, user interfaces are very important to detect the user intention, which is critical to define goals for the wheelchair to be able to assist him/her.
- People presenting mostly cognitive impairments may require a different kind of assistive aids, which may lead even a more relevant role in the sharing of personal autonomy. In this scenario the user probably does not have very clear goals or is not capable of achieving them because he/she cannot remember *how* to do them. In these cases, AT may empower and complement their autonomy using agents that offer them a set of services, like reminding what kind of activities they can or should perform at a certain moment of the day or pointing them out how to achieve these activities. The main idea is to offer the users a set of cognitive aids, either rational or memory based, that can ease their daily living.

Multi-agent systems have both the flexibility and the cognitive capabilities required in order to be able to support the needs of persons with different disability profiles and to complement the autonomy of the people with special needs in an adaptive way through the time. In some cases the disability is a consequence of a pathology or a trauma, that may improve with some time and rehabilitation. An excess of support or lack of flexibility in the support can make this process more difficult, on the other hand an assistance adaptive to the daily state of the patient may be helpful in the rehabilitation process.

Some patients may dislike an autonomous navigation system, or choosing among a set of maneuvers, they may prefer driving by themselves, to feel autonomous and in charge of the situation at all times. An intelligent agent with the necessary knowledge of a user's profile can supervise user's navigation and take part in some driving maneuvers, in a transparent way, in case the user needs some support (e.g., help crossing doorways, refining turning maneuvers, help keeping stable cruise navigation, ...). A model like the one presented in Fig 1 would apply progressive support in the control, from none to full, depending on the navigation situation (corridor navigation, doorway cross, following a route,...) the quality of control (is turning correctly around the corner? is getting too close to the wall?...) and the user's status.

In order to make this possible the user's agent must have to have deep knowledge of the user's disability profile and historical data about his/her driving behaviour, merge all this knowledge and translate it in control support and a set of assistive services. All this knowledge and information must be updated dynamically, since the user can progress in either good or bad way or just can have a

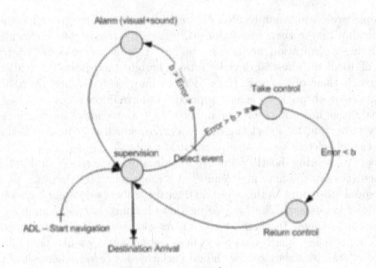

FIGURE 1. Control evolution graph in navigation

good/bad day driving-wise. The knowledge learnt by each agent would be shared and distributed among other agents that have users with similar profiles so they can take advantage of the experiences traced by the first one. As shown in Fig 2 agent's responsibility grows when the measure of his active intervention in the user's autonomy is exerted. This means a heavier charge of *obligations* regarding safety and soundness in the undertaken actions.

Most important among the main open issues in shared autonomy – the ones we identify as crucial – are those related with the assessment of disruptive and/or unexpected events where the system has to act proactively but also in a safe and sound way for the user.

The trust of a user, a caregiver, a medical specialist or a nurse in their own *agent* – a personal assistant – is a prerequisite to delegate part of their responsibilities to it [10]. The personalized ways of communication with their own *agent* is a first step to build this confidence. Augmenting the communication facilities is enhancing the patient's ways of interacting with environment and therefore augmenting user's QoL.

Among the characteristics we expect from such a systems we have:

- *intelligent information gathering*: the system should be able not only to receive the different information inputs (but also to reason about the knowledge it has about the state of the user or the environment (resulting from the interpretation of information, see next item), what information they need to improve their knowledge (e.g., to assess the user condition), where to get it, and how to get it.

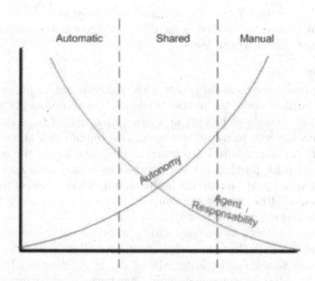

FIGURE 2. Autonomy-responsibility relationship

- *information combination and interpretation*: one or several pieces of data should be combined and translated into a meaningful piece of information. As both the condition of the user and the state of the environment may change in time, interpretation of a piece of data may not only change depending on the point of view (the users', the institution's or the environment's point of view) but also from the current condition of the user and the state of the environment. A special case is the interpretation of information in order to detect a dangerous condition of the patient (e.g., patient fell out of the wheelchair) or a dangerous state of the environment (e.g., fire detection) which will trigger an alarm in the system.
- *information filtering and intelligent distribution*: depending on relevance of the information they receive, the middleware should completely or partially filter the information and then distribute it to the different components that may need such information. A special case is alarm distribution during emergencies, where information needed to handle the emergency (e.g., evacuation planning) is prioritised over other information during the emergency situation.

We live in an environment where the available infrastructure for communications is more reliable and rapidly growing. Several classes of communication and collaborative applications are appearing but they are far from being easily integrable among them [7]. Many efforts are made towards the adoption of a common reference architecture for the development of clinically significant health telematic services.

We see here a niche for intelligent agents to be used as interfaces among them. An important issue to be tackled is the design of general interfaces that have the ability to adapt themselves to users.

2.1. Scenarios

Devices have been used to *assist* people with cognitive and/or physical disabilities to complete various tasks for almost 20 years. What represents a change and challenge is the abilities embedded in a new generation of tools that are able to cooperate with the user to complete a task. This implies that these new tools are context-aware and are able to learn from the interaction with the user.

Cooperation for problem solving between users and their *agent* and the cooperation between *agents* among themselves requires some kind of model which at least describes *what to expect from whom* in terms of questions, actions, etc and that uses previous experiences and trust.

Scenarios appear to be an easy and appropriate way to create partitions of the world and to relate them with time. Scenarios allow actions to be performed in a given time. For example, Mihailidis *et al.*, in [1], studied the *handwashing* scenario where a full instrumented environment was used to provide users with cues to support the completion of this task.

As in Mihalilidis' approach we are looking to support those tasks that are needed to perform the most important Activities of Daily Life (ADL). In particular, those related with mobility but not only.

3. The experiment and sample population

In order to grant more autonomy and self-dependency to the target users, it is crucial to ease their mobility problems. In [3] we explained a MAS that could autonomously navigate through an environment carrying a user, a prototype that improves the notion of freedom and autonomy of the users. On the other hand, introducing the concept of *shared control* augments self-dependency in the user and this is another benefit of the project. We designed our new prototype with this idea in mind, a robotic wheelchair that chooses between navigating autonomously or granting the control to the user, depending on the user profile and local behaviour. Importance on rehabilitation aspects of this approach must be noted.

3.1. Related work

Research has given much attention to assistive wheelchairs like SENARIO (Sensor Aided Intelligent Wheelchair Navigation System) [4], Wheelesley, SIAMO, Rolland, Navchair or Smartchair [31, 15]. All these systems share some common features: a set of sensors, some processing unit and the software to decide *what to do*.

The first autonomous wheelchairs [8] simply provided a basic set of primitives like AvoidObstacle, FollowWall and PassDoorway to assist the person in difficult manoeuvres. In most cases, these primitives were manually selected by the users.

Futher systems like MAID (Mobile Aid for Elderly and Disabled people), NavChair [27], TinMan [21], Smartchair [25] were mostly based on the subsumption architecture [5]. In these cases, rather than manual selection, events detected by onboard sensors triggered one or several behaviours. These behaviours were merged, according to some rules, into an emergent one. The main difference among these systems is how behaviours are implemented. In some cases, the user does not guide the chair at all, but simply provides a destination [28]. Some of these systems let the user override control whenever he/she wants to [21]. For safety reasons, in some cases the wheelchair may also override the human use and select a behaviour on its own [27, 14].

3.2. The Technical Test

The experiment consisted in instructing each one of the users to go from A to B ($\overline{AB}$) following a simple straight line drawn on the floor using a wheelchair. The maximum speed of the wheelchair has been fixed as described. The experiment evaluates the performance of the navigation using a conventional wheelchair, an electrically powered wheelchair and finally the autonomous wheelchair prototype with *shared control*. The hypothesis is that our MAS will support the user to finalize this task safely. Also, we like to measure the user's acceptance of the *shared control*. Here we describe the three tests that were performed by a group of inpatients of IRCCS. All subjects gave written informed consent to participate in the study, and the protocol was approved by the IRCCS ethical committee. We do not know other experiments like this performed in real inpatients.

3.2.1. Test 1: conventional wheelchair.
The first test consisted in a simple task for the user: To follow a straight line drawn on the floor strolling their own conventional wheelchair. Since this chair was not equipped with any kind of sensor no numerical data was retrieved. The aim of this test was to subjectively evaluate the user's performance and driving abilities.

3.2.2. Test 2: powered wheelchair – manual control.
In the second test, the user was provided with an electrically-powered wheelchair to follow a different equivalent straight line of Test 1, to avoid learning effect. As with all conventional electrically-powered wheelchair the control was executed with the use of a joystick. The wheelchair used was the *SHARE-it* robotic prototype, described in Figure 8, set up in passive mode, which left all the control to the user and used all the attached sensors to store data about the test performance. Different data was collected into a log like absolute position, orientation, speed and joystick commands. The execution of the test was monitored all the time to ensure the safety of the users, having the hardware emergency stop remote command just in case any risk could arise.

3.2.3. Test 3: powered wheelchair – shared control.
The third test was executed on another equivalent traced line to avoid learning factor using the robotic wheelchair with *shared control*. In this setting $\overline{AB}$ is well-located in a map that is served by

the *ha* to the user's *pa* and, therefore, we assume that the user has the *intention* of going from A to B following as closely as possible the traced line in. At the beginning of each driving the *ha* grants permission to start each individual user as s/he is authorized to stroll in the garden, as explained in Section 4.3.

A set of thresholds was defined relating the distance between the wheelchair and the line. Those thresholds are adapted to each driving situation. While the wheelchair is located in a distance below the first threshold (green zone), the user has full control of the mobile. If the user moves away from the line surpassing the first threshold, he enters the second zone (yellow zone) where keeps full control of the wheelchair but receives visual and sound signal alarms to make him learn that he is getting away from the traced route and must correct the driving. If the user keeps moving away from the line and the second threshold is surpassed, the wheelchair enters the third zone (red zone). When, from the sensor information, the *pa* detects that the wheelchair has entered into the red zone, it takes the total control of the navigation driving it, smoothly, back to the green zone to avoid stress on the user's behaviour. When the *pa* has the control all joystick commands are ignored, but still they are recorded for later analysis. On Figure 3 you can see the thresholds.

3.3. Test and Results

3.3.1. Sample Population. Participants in this study were recruited among neurological and orthopaedic inpatients who needed a daily use of wheelchair consecutively admitted at the IRCCS in Rome, Italy, during a four-week period. Exclusion criteria in patient selection were: patients bedridden, patients walking autonomously, presence of global aphasia, blindness. A group of 24/31 patients was selected: 10 males (41.7%) and 14 females (58.3%); mean age 67.7 years. Each subject underwent a structured clinical evaluation and an assessment of cognitive, emotional and functional abilities. The entire procedure was performed by a trained physician. *Cognitive Assessment* was measured by the Mini Mental State Examination (MMSE) [12] scale. MMSE is a well-established, reliable, and valid brief cognitive screening instrument that has a high inter-rater reliability and is easy to administer. Each subscale is scored up to a total score of 30 points for optimal performance. Cognitive impairment is defined according to the standard cut-off as a score ≤ 24 points. *Emotional Assessment* was measured by the Geriatric Depression Scale, 15-item version (GDS-15, abridged from [26]). This scale was developed as a basic screening measure for depression in older adults. It is easy to administer, needs no prior psychiatric knowledge and has been well validated in many environments - home and clinical. Scoring Intervals: 0-5 No depression; 6-10 Mild depression; 11+ Severe depression. *Functional Assessment* was measured by The Barthel-Index [17]. The Barthel-Index (B.I.) was used to assess the activity of daily living in 10 areas (feeding, transfers bed to chair and back, grooming, toilet use, bathing, mobility, climbing stairs, dressing, stool control, bladder control); the maximal score is 100 points.

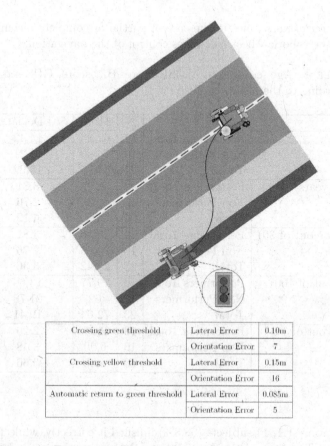

Crossing green threshold	Lateral Error	0.10m
	Orientation Error	7
Crossing yellow threshold	Lateral Error	0.15m
	Orientation Error	16
Automatic return to green threshold	Lateral Error	0.085m
	Orientation Error	5

FIGURE 3. Thresholds on shared control

In Test 1 the users who were not able to complete the trajectory and/or stopped the test have been considered as *non performers* . In Test 2 those users have been considered as *non performers* who stopped the test and those who finished the test but were located in the higher quartile with respect to:

1. number of failures done during the route;
2. total time (sec) taken to perform the test;
3. time while failure (%) during the route;
4. Root Mean Square Error (RMSE)

The higher quartile has been chosen to define *non performers* to classify a group of subjects with an ineffective performance, in absence of cut-off thresholds or reference values in literature.

A *failure* in the execution of the experiment has been detected when the center of the wheelchair is situated beyond 0.15 meters from the drawn line (crossing the yellow threshold) or the orientation error grows higher than 16°. In Test 3 there were no *non performers*, since in the case of partial or complete incompetence of the subject, the robotic wheelchair takes control of the navigation.

TABLE 1. Age, education, MMSE score, B.I. score, GDS score, according to the results of Test 1

		N	Mean	Std Deviation	Sig
Age (years)	Performers Total	14	62,86	14,42	
	Non Performers	10	74,60	14,21	0,061
	Total	24	67,75	15,22	
Education (years)	Performers Total	14	8,79	3,81	
	Non Performers	10	9,70	2,76	0,604
	Total	24	9,17	4,12	
MMSE (score out of 30)	Performers Total	13	25,86	3,81	
	Non Performers	10	24,86	2,76	0,494
	Total	23	25,42	3,36	
B.I. (score out of 100)	Performers Total	13	79,77	13,66	
	Non Performers	10	62	21,78	0,026
	Total	23	72,04	19,41	
GDS (score out of 15)	Performers Total	13	2,38	2,26	
	Non Performers	10	6,90	3,48	0,001
	Total	23	4,35	3,60	

3.4. Results

With regard to Test 1, 14 subjects (58,3%) finished it correctly, while 12 subjects (50%) finished Test 2 correctly. According to the reasons reported above, Test 3 has been finished correctly by all the 24 subjects as expected.

Table 1 reports age, education, MMSE score, B.I. score, GDS score, according to the results of Test 1. Table 2 reports age, education, MMSE score, B.I. score, GDS score, according to the results of Test 2. The t-test for the difference of means was used and it was accepted a statistical significance of 0.05.

4. SHARE-it: Agent-based Supported Human Autonomy

In a first approach to a prototype implementation of the *SHARE-it* project [9], we have only partially developed some of the elements of its three layered architecture (see Figure 4). The third level, in red on the top, corresponds to the MAS. MAS provide a framework in which a set of autonomous, intelligent, flexible, proactive and reactive programs (agents) may communicate and co-operate to solve complex problems in distributed settings. MAS offer an implementation alternative that certainly fits *SHARE-it* needs, because they exhibit the following interesting properties:

TABLE 2. Age, education, MMSE score, B.I. score, GDS score, according to the results of Test 2

		N	Mean	Std Deviation	Sig
Age (years)	Performers Total	12	65	15,92	
	Non Performers	12	70,50	14,63	0,388
	Total	24	67,75	15,21	
Education (years)	Performers Total	12	9,5	4,25	
	Non Performers	12	8,83	4,15	0,701
	Total	24	9,17	4,12	
MMSE (score out of 30)	Performers Total	12	26,81	2,07	
	Non Performers	11	23,92	2,92	0,036
	Total	23	25,42	3,36	
B.I. (score out of 100)	Performers Total	12	77,75	19,25	
	Non Performers	11	65,82	18,44	0,145
	Total	23	72,04	19,41	
GDS (score out of 15)	Performers Total	12	3,42	3,18	
	Non Performers	11	5,36	3,91	0,202
	Total	23	4,35	3,60	

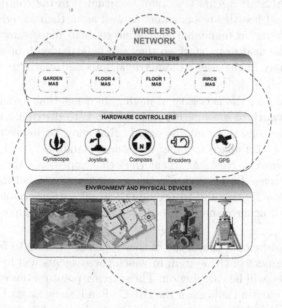

FIGURE 4. The *SHARE-it* proposed multi-level architecture.

- *Modularity*: the different services or functionalities may be distributed among diverse agents, depending on their complexity. This also make each component easily reusable (see Section 4.2).

- *Efficiency*: agents may coordinate their activities to perform complex tasks, so that several parts of the same process may be solved concurrently by different agents executing on different hosts.
- *Reliability*: any distributed process is more reliable than its centralised counterpart, because there does not exist a single point of failure that may cause the crash of the whole system at once.
- *Flexibility*: agents may be dynamically created or eliminated according to the needs of the application. Negotiation and knowledge exchange allow the optimisation of shared resources.

Our MAS has implemented the following basic agents. Firstly, we have the *Patient Agent* (*pa*), that will run in a PDA or a Ultra-Mobile PC (UMPC). An instantiation of this agent should provide all the available and permitted services to each patient, from now on user, and it should take care of his/hers personal security. Each pa_i provides a personalized way of interaction with the user and therefore users could use it to ask for help or to ask the platform to drive her/him to a given place into the permitted space or to ask the system to show a possible path to the destination. Also, the *pa* takes under its responsibility the audit of the user's biometric signals and depending on its readings takes some actions.

The *Medical Staff Agents* (*ma*) will be situated in the computers belonging to the medical and healthcare personnel as well as in their individual PDA. The *ma* will be in charge of managing all the user's help request messages and will notify them to the healthcare staff, so they can be attended properly. Also, it will notify any anomaly in the user's biometric signals and it will generate a request for help, if needed.

We also consider the necessity of having an agent that undertakes responsibility for the network of sensors. Its basic target is to distribute the information from all available sensors to all the agents that may be interested. The list of actual sensors for this space include: movement, landmarks, cameras, presence, etc. Finally, we have a *Hospital Agent* (*ha*) that represents the hospital entity. Among its objectives are to maintain the monitorisation of all users, to manage their daily living activities and to provide them all with the mobility plans that may be needed to achieve them. Also, it reports possible failures in the network of sensors.

In order to develop a prototype of these agents, we have to take in consideration the environment of the system in which these agents will be *living* together and the tasks they will be carrying on. The starting point for our experiment environment are the garden facilities of the IRCCS Fondazione Santa Lucia, a hospital for Neuromotor Rehabilitation located in Rome. In this hospital garden we can find different walkway routes usually used by the users. This is the physical environment where our *SHARE-it* agents will be working. We must remark that we are producing the design of a MAS where agents that run over a physical platform –like the robotic wheelchairs – and the agents that run in the multi-agent platform and only receive inputs from other agents (human or software), will be coexisting.

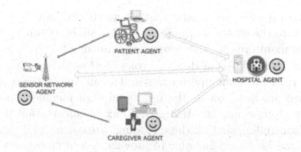

FIGURE 5. The *e*-tools-V2 MAS

4.1. Architecture

To create the description and specification of the MAS level of the *e*-tools-V2 architecture, we use the GAIA [30] methodology. In this architecture we find the typical
elements that shape a platform of agents as the FIPA [11] understands it. This includes an Agent Directory service, to register and to locate the agents, a Services
Directory, that allows to register the services that the agents of the system offer
and, finally, a Message Transport System that establishes the necessary infrastructure for the agent communication. These communications are always carried
out using the same interaction language between agents, the FIPA Agent Communication Language (ACL), and the communicative protocols described by the
FIPA.

4.1.1. Roles. Following the preliminary description of the agents that we presented
previously, we will detail in here some of the roles that each of the agent prototypes can assume. Entering in the detailed analysis of each agent, we start with
the *pa*. In our first experiment, see [2], the *pa* development was more focused on
the monitoring and control of the robotic wheelchair, so for this garden test we
have renamed it Wheelchair Agent. It interprets roles involved in a *Help Request
Manager* so to ask for help, with direct interaction or not of the user. The role
of *Plan Request Manager* to communicate with someone that can provide him a
route in the environment for traveling between two points. The role of *Monitoring
Manager* keeps control of the wheelchair status, in future prototypes where biometric technology will be included, users' vital constants will be monitored and
assured that they have acceptable readings. Finally, we have the *Navigator/Plan
Executioner* that is in charge of managing the journey marked by a route in the
environment.

The *ma* play roles of *Help Attend Manager* that allows them to pay attention
to those requests of help that the *pas* have processed, managing their solution. On
the other hand it develops the role of *Status Request Manager* that allows to make
a follow-up of the detailed information regarding the users. This information could
be biometrical data that helps to identify the user (i.e., fingerprints), medical data
that indicates the user's status (heartbeats, temperature, blood pressure,...) as

well as personal or geographical data, that allows the *ma* to have located the user at all times. Due to the sensor configuration and availability only the geographical information was monitored for the garden experiment.

The Sensor Network Agent develops roles of *Monitoring*, since it picks up all the sensory information of our environment and it can control the *reported/detected* changes that are produced on it, the users and staff members' positions, doors that open up and close up, *etc.* Using this flux of information it performs the task of *Guard*, controlling that all these readings are correct and that there are no anomalies that can be considered able to provoke risk or emergency situations. In our garden experiment this agent was implemented as a variable server agent that recorded and distributed the wheelchair data and sensor readings.

The *ha* develops roles of coordination and control of the system. For example, it controls the actions of *Monitoring* and *Guard* in order to survey the user's data and to control that they are correct, as well as keeping track of any reported incidence. It also carries out the *Planner* role, since it receives requests from the *pa* and calculates the *best* route in the environment. Finally, it will have the role of *Scheduler* or agenda, so it is in charge of carrying out the control of the activities that users have to carry out along the day and of warning them when the time of their attending has arrived. For our experiment a very limited version of the agenda was implemented, only to record the Activities of Daily Life (ADL)[2] regarding the garden walk.

The agents that act in our architecture share an ontology that allows them to exchange information for carrying out their activities. This ontology contains the description of the elements of the physical environment as well as those of the conceptual world that the agents need to know. It also contains the actions and propositions that give support to the communicative acts that put them in contact. This early prototype ontology has been coded using the Protégé environment [24].

4.2. Services

Now, we have already introduced some of the agents that take part in our MAS platform, even though not all their services have been implemented at this stage. Once we have defined the agents of our system and their roles, we are able to see their participation in the services that *e-tools-V2* offers. One of these services is related to the user's needs for attention. The *Help Request* service allows the user to ask for help whenever he needs it, propagating a notification to all the *ma* so the caregivers can choose to answer this help request using the *Help Attend* service or leave the request in a queue. Also, this *Help Request* can be produced automatically, through the monitoring service that keeps control of the user's vital constants in the *pa*, that when it believes that these data readings are abnormal, it autonomously warns the *ma* about these irregularities. Special biometrical sensors need to be installed to perform this service in future versions of the system.

---

[2] ADL y AT

Following the monitoring line we also find the *Emergency* service, that is provided by the agent of the sensors network. This service works by taking continuous care of some sensors, controlling that situations of risk or emergency may not arise. Among the signals to be controlled we are considering electrical, fire, smoke, *etc.* If the detected situation, a combination of abnormal signals, is considered an emergency, the system would proceed to an automatic evacuation of the users, bringing them to the closest safe location from their current positions, always following the designed protocols of the institution for these situations.

The *ma* agents have the possibility to use the *Request Status* service to update all the user's information. Medical and positional data is susceptible to change with time. Thanks to the updated medical data the healthcare staff will be able to read through their *ma* the status of their patients' vital constants and follow their evolution. Also, when an automatic *request of help* may rise by abnormal readings in these biomedical data, the healthcare staff could browse on-line which are these readings and if it is necessary, they could collect the medical material that they may need before visiting the user. Furthermore, making use of the position information that this service provides, the system will know at anytime where the users can be found, if they are standing or in movement and in the latter case, the system may know where they are heading to, since probably it has planned the route.

The *Scheduling* service is meant to improve, to a certain degree, the afore mentioned user's cognitive problems. Often users suffering this impairment do forget which are their daily living activities (*ADLs*), as for example that they have to go to the dinning room to have lunch, or to go to the gymnasium to make their exercises, *etc.* That is why e-tools-V2 offers them an agenda service that *knows* all their *ADLs*. When, in a given moment, the *ha* detects that a user has a programmed activity in a given location, it warns his *pa*, that will be entrusted to warn his owner and will offer him the possibility to drive him to the place where the appointment is taking place. If the appointment is not compulsory and the user refuses to attend in that moment, his *pa* will remind him later that he still has a pending appointment.

Finally, we present the mobility service. Using the *Planning* service the user can ask the system to drive him to a specific zone of the hospital or can just ask to be reminded of how to reach a destination, in the case he has forgotten. The user can choose, through the interface that his *pa* offers, to which room he wants to travel. We must say that the *pa* will be only offering him as options, those rooms to which he can have access, and will avoid stairs, private rooms, offices, *etc.* Once the user has selected his destination, his *pa* gets in touch with the *ha* and requests a route to go from the actual position to the chosen destination. When the *ha* receives the request, it calculates the appropriate route in the way that we will portray later. Once it has the resulting route, it sends it like a list of points to attain within a message back to the *pa* that had made the request. When the *pa* receives the route, it starts to execute it automatically, showing it to the user through the interface. The user will be able to actively interact with the controls of the chair, and if he prefers so, he can be the one who manually follows the points marked by the route.

To create plans, initially the *ha* needs a map of the environment to be able to design them. In our case we are using the real map of a floor of the Hospital Santa Lucia, we divided it into sections or stretches to convert it into a topological map. The topological map observes the geometric relations between the detected characteristics in the map with respect to an arbitrary axis of reference. This is represented as a graph where the nodes are the observed characteristics (rooms, room sections, *etc.*) and the edges are the relations between them. These maps can be constructed without a reference to the actual position of the platform. Therefore the errors of representation are independent of the positioning errors of the platform.

In our particular case we have divided the map into a grid and have drawn a graph that connects the stretches that can be safe or useful for the users to travel. The edges will indicate the associated cost to the transition from a stretch to the next. The nodes also have an associated cost related to crossing the stretch associated. Places like corridors, narrow zones or doors suppose an added cost. Edges only connect stretches that are physically connected and that are transitable. Once we have the topological map, from the start node and the destination node, we have to calculate the best route. In order to obtain it, we will make use of the well-known A* algorithm, that provides us with the optimum route in cost and efficient time.

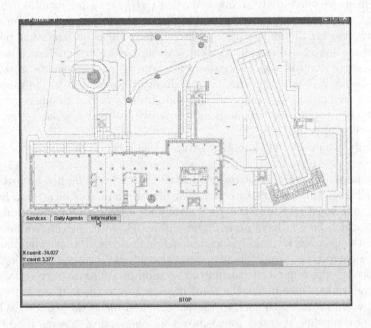

FIGURE 6. Plan execution on Patient Agent

The system will modify the topological map that we have loaded in memory. When it calculates a route and assigns it to a Patient$_A$, immediately, it will mark all sections of the map that he will use, increasing its cost, so that if any other Patient$_B$ asks for a route, the system will try to search for an alternative path, in order to not use sections already assigned to Patient$_A$. Once Patient$_A$ reaches her destination, the sections will be modified again and leave them with their initial costs. This strategy is meant to diminish possible traffic jams. This dynamic modification of the sections cost is also useful for the system when it has to cope with closed doors or blocked accesses. As the ha modifies the costs of transition from a section to another it will not try to pass for those temporarily closed accesses.

Although safety and soundness are not services by themselves, they must be present in all the afore mentioned services. With safety we do not only cover physical risks, but also ethical issues are considered protecting the integrity and privacy of users data in all the information exchanges. Safety will be an implicit layer in the ha ensuring that users only access safe and allowed areas of the facilities, monitoring their position all the time, forbidding navigation requests to restricted locations and stopping the wheelchair when close to hazardous places like stairs, steps, or non-driveable surfaces like grass. Safety also considers battery checks, to ensure that users can reach their location when they want to execute a plan; this situation is crucial when trying to execute an emergency plan [13].

4.3. Implementation

In this paper we focused on one of the most common assistive devices adopted for mobility limitations and their correlates: the wheelchair. Unfortunately the wheelchair is one of the most difficult to use autonomously (requiring control, physical interaction and also planning/strategy for navigation or obstacle avoidance). One possible solution is represented by the use of power wheelchairs, but the extreme difficulty with which persons with severe disabilities are taught to manoeuvre a power wheelchair is an example of difficult interaction with Assistive Technologies (AT): 9 to 10% of patients who receive power wheelchair training find it extremely difficult or impossible to use the wheelchair for ADL; 40% of patients reported difficult or impossible steering and manoeuvring tasks; 85% of clinicians

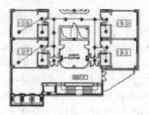

FIGURE 7. The topologic map

reported that a number of patients lack the required motor skills, strength, or visual acuity. Nearly half of the patients unable to control a power wheelchair by conventional methods would benefit from an automated navigation system.

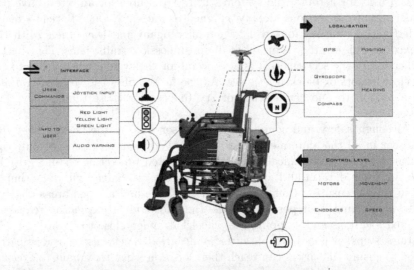

FIGURE 8. Sensors and actuators of the wheelchair

With e-tools-V2 we developed a navigation test with real users in the IRCCS garden facilities, to evaluate their interaction with the system and to make a step forward in the development of the modules and services enclosed in the *SHARE-it* project. All subjects gave written informed consent for participation to the study, and the protocol was approved by the IRCCS Fondazione Santa Lucia ethical committee.

For this we have implemented a first working version of the *SHARE-it ha* consisting of simplified versions of *pa*, *ha* and sensor network agent. This reduced *ha* allowed users to dock their *pa* into the agent platform to perform a garden walk. Before this could be done, the *pa* requested *ha* an ADL check to ensure that the user was allowed to perform such activity, making use of a simplified agenda developed for the experiment. Once the *pa* was authorized to use the wheelchair, a technician representing the user, selected a destination for the walk route among the available set, and after calculating the navigation plan, the *pa* started executing the walk sending movement commands to the wheelchair hardware controllers. The early development stage of the *pa* is not yet focused on interfaces for persons with disabilities. This is the reason for the technician interacting with the *pa* rather than the user, just to focus them on the navigation experience instead of adding more stress trying to understand the agent interface.

This agent framework is the one we used on the execution of the experiment described in Section 3, being the *pa* in charge of the shared control administration.

5. Conclusion

Current trends in healthcare, at least at European Union level, call for integrated user-oriented telematic services, which ensure prompt and secure access to information resources, provided proper authorization is available. We claim that such services should be personalized and mediated by a MAS owned by the user herself.

It must be observed that Personalization through Ambient Intelligence is a key issue in this Vision. AmI implies three relatively new technologies: Ubiquitous Computation, Ubiquitous Communication, and Intelligent User Interfaces.

In this sense our idea is to introduce AT in existing older people's housing in order to provide *Intermediate care* [19] intended as the range of services designed to facilitate transition from hospital to home, and from medical dependence to functional independence; where the objectives of care are not primarily medical, the patients' discharge can be anticipated as well.

There is a strong case for the use of *SHARE-it* and, therefore, intelligent agents to support mobility and communication in senior citizens. Moreover, there is a clear evolutionary pathway that will take us from current AT to more widespread AmI where MAS will be kernel for interaction and support for decision-making. In our view the user should be assisted according to his/her profile: not more, not less.

5.1.

Real world experiments, real environment, and real users– to probe the validity and appropriateness of AT marks a new step forward in its deploying. The use of Agent Technology in this field is opening new ways of interaction and creating new solutions. The ultimate goal of the interaction between robotics, Agent Systems and the user is to enhance autonomy and up-grade the quality and complexity of services offered. Nevertheless, some important topics as safeness and security have to be redefined in the future in order to broaden the applicability of this approach[13]. An open topic is the acceptability of this technology. Senior citizens facing some disabilities need to find this technology easy to learn as well as be confident with its usage in their preferred environment. This implies an effort to provide the appropriate infrastructure else-where. Also, it should be easy to adapt this technological solutions to different environments.

References

[1] Geoff R. Ferniea Alex Mihailidisa, ? and William L. Cleghornb. The development of a computerized cueing device to help people with dementia to be more independent. *Technology and Disability*, 13(1):23–40, 2000.

[2] C. Barrué, L. Céspedes, U. Cortés, R. Annicchiarico, and C. Caltagirone. e- toolsv1: The agent level. In *Proceedings of 2nd ECAI Workshop on Agents Applied in Health Care*, pages 55–61, 2004.

[3] Cristian Barrué, Ulises Cortés, Antonio B. Martínez, Josep Escoda, Roberta Annicchiarico, and Carlo Caltagirone. -tools: An agent coordination layer to support the mobility of persons with disabilities. In *IFIP AI*, pages 425–434, 2006.

[4] G. Bourhis, O.Horn, O.Habert, and A.Pruski. An autonomous vehicle for people with motor disabilities. *IEEE Robotics & Automation Magazine*, 8:20–28, 2001.

[5] R.A. Brooks. Intelligence without Reason. In *Proceedings of the 8th. Int. Joint Conf. on Artificial Intelligence. Sydney, Australia.*, pages 569–595, 1991.

[6] L.M. Camarinha-Matos and H. Afasarmanesh. *Virtual communities and elderly support*, pages 279–284. WSES, 2001.

[7] P. J. Clarke, V. Hristidis, Y. Wang, N. Prabakar, and Y. Deng. A declarative approach for specifying user-centric communication. In *Symposium on Collaborative Technologies and Systems*, 2006.

[8] Jonathan H. Connell and Paul Viola. Cooperative control of a semi-autonomous mobile robot. In *Proceedings of the IEEE Conference on Robotics and Automation, Cincinnati*, 1990.

[9] U. Cortés, R. Annicchiarico, J. Vázquez-Salceda, C. Urdiales, L. Cañamero, M. López, M. Sànchez-Marrè, and C. Caltagirone. Assistive technologies for the disabled and for the new generation of senior citizens: the e-Tools architecture. *AI Communications*, 16:193–207, 2003.

[10] G. de Haan, O. Blanson Henkemans, M.A. Neerincx, and C.A.P.G. van der Mast. SuperAssist: Personal assistants for diabetes healthcare treatment at home. In *Home-Oriented Informatics and Telematics (Hoit'05)*, pages 261–275. IFIP, 2005.

[11] FIPA 2000 Specification. http://www.fipa.org/repository/fipa2000.html.

[12] F. Folstein, S. E. Folstein, and P. R. McHugh. Mini-mental state. a practical method for grading the cognitive state of patients for the clinician. *J Am Geriatr Soc*, 12:189–198, 1975.

[13] J. Fox and S. Das. *Safe and Sound: Artificial Intelligence in Hazardous Applications*. AAAI Press/MIT Press, 1st edition, 2000.

[14] T. Gomi and A Griffith. *Developing Intelligent Wheelchairs for the Handicapped*, pages 150–178. Springer Verlag, 1998.

[15] A. Lankenau and T. Röfer. Smart wheelchairs - state of the art in an emerging market.

[16] A. Lankenau and T. Röfer. The role of shared control in service robots - the bremen autonomous wheelchair as an example. In *Service Robotics - Applications and Safety Issues in an Emerging Market. Workshop Notes*, pages 27–31, 2000.

[17] F. I. Mahoney and D. W. Barthel. Functional evaluation: The barthel index. *Md State Med J.*, 14:61–65, 1965.

[18] D.W.K. Man, E.W.T. Lee, and E.C.H. Tong. Health services needs and quality of life assessment of individuals with brain injuries: a pilot cross-sectional study. *Brain Injury*, 18(6):577–591, 2004.

[19] R.J. Melis, M.G. Olde Rikkert, S.G. Parker, and M.I. van Eijken. What is intermediate care? *BMJ*, 329:360–361, 2004.

[20] A. Mihailidis, P. Elinas, Daniel Gunn, J. Boger, and J. Hoey. Profile of disability in elderly people: estimates from a longitudinal population study. *UbiHealth 2006:*

The *4th International Workshop on Ubiquitous Computing for Pervasive Healthcare Applications*, 2006.

[21] D.P. Miller and M.G. Slack. Design & testing of a low-cost robotic wheelchair. *Autonomous Robots*, 1(3), 1995.

[22] V.O. Mittal, H.A. Yanco, J. Aronis, and R. Simpson, editors. *Assistive Technology and Artificial Intelligence: Applications in Robotics, User Interfaces and Natural Language Processing*, volume 1458 of *Lecture Notes in Artificial Intelligence*. Springer-Verlag, Berlin, 1998.

[23] M. E. Polack. Intelligent Technology for an Aging Population: The use of AI to assist elders with cognitive impairment. *AI Magazine*, 26(2):9–24, 2005.

[24] FIPA 2000 Specification: The Protégé Ontology Editor and Knowledge Acquisition System. http://protege.stanford.edu/.

[25] R. S. Rao, K. Conn, S. H. Jung, J. Katupitiya, T. Kientz, V. Kumar, J. Ostrowski, S. Patel, and C. J. Taylor. Human robot interaction: Applications to smart wheelchairs. In *Proceedings of the IEEE Conference on Robotics and Automation, Washington*, 2002.

[26] R.L. Sheikh and J.A. Yesavage. Geriatric depression scale (gds). recent evidence and development of a shorter version. *Clinical Gerontologist*, 5:165–73, 1968.

[27] R. Simpson and S.P. Levine. *NavChair: An Assistive Wheelchair Navigation System with Automatic Adaptation*, pages 235–255. Springer-Verlag, 1998.

[28] R. C. Simpson and S.P. Levine. Voice control of a powered wheelchair. *IEEE Trans Neural Syst Rehabil Eng.*, 10(2):122–125, 2002.

[29] D. Vanhooydonck, E. Demeester, M. Nuttin, and H. Van Brussel. Shared control for intelligent wheelchairs: an implicit estimation of the user intention. In *Proceedings of the 1st International Workshop on Advances in Service Robotics 2003*, 2003.

[30] Michael Wooldridge, Nicholas R. Jennings, and David Kinny. The gaia methodology for agent-oriented analysis and design. *Autonomous Agents and Multi-Agent Systems*, 3(3):285–312, 2000.

[31] H.A. Yanco. Integrating robotic research: a survey of robotic wheelchair development. In H.A. Yanco, editor, *AAAI Spring Symposium on Integrating Robotic Research*. AAAI, AAAI., 1998.

Ulises Cortés
Technical University of Catalonia
Omega 135. Jordi Girona 1 & 3
Barcelona 08034
Spain
e-mail: ia@lsi.upc.edu

Roberta Annicchiarico
Fondazione Santa Lucia
Via Ardetina 354
Roma, Italia
e-mail: r.annicchiarico@hsantalucia.it

Cristina Urdiales
University of Malaga
Departamento Tecnología Electrónica, E.T.S.I. Telecomunicación, Campus de Teatinos
29071 Málaga
Spain
e-mail: `acurdiales@uma.es`

Cristian Barrué and Antonio Martínez
Technical University of Catalonia
Omega s206. Jordi Girona 1 & 3
Barcelona 08034
Spain
e-mail: `cbarrue@lsi.upc.edu`
       `antonio.b.martinez@upc.edu`

Alfredo Villar
IBM
Barcelona 080
Spain
e-mail: `alfredo.villar@es.ibm.com`

Carlo Caltagirone
Fondazione Santa Lucia
Via Ardetina 354
Roma, Italia
e-mail: `c.caltagirone@hsantalucia.it`

Whitestein Series in Software Agent Technologies and Autonomic Computing, 141–148
© 2007 Birkhäuser Verlag Basel/Switzerland

Agents and Healthcare: A Glance to the Future

Alfredo Villar, Alessia Federici and Roberta Annicchiarico

1. Introduction

The global expansion of information technologies in every sector and industry made the use of computers in Health-care increasingly common since long time ago. Recently new and innovative applications of information technologies in Health-care are going up in several areas.

There are new applications around e-Health[1]. Computerized data management is also becoming increasingly important in clinical practice and research. Managed care offers the promise of more integrated services, including those related with preventive care and support maintenance of independence at the lowest level of care. Areas that have attracted attention so far include:

- *Home Care* where a large number of *eHealth* services, basically telematic services, have been tested.
- *Pre-Hospital Emergency Care* where telematic tools and services are combined for optimal planning, and response management to health emergencies.
- *Hospital Care* where autonomous laboratory and clinical information systems have been coordinated to give support to clinical decision making. Including the development of Electronic Health Records (HER) that provide a decentralized view of the patient's medical record by dynamically composing

---

Authors would like to acknowledge support from the *SHARE-it*: Supported Human Autonomy for Recovery and Enhancement of cognitive and motor abilities using information technologies (FP6-IST-045088). The views expressed in this paper are not necessarily those of *SHARE-it* consortium.

[1]The term was apparently first used by industry leaders and marketing people rather than academics (coming from e-commerce, e-business, e-solutions, an so on). One of the most accept definition is written by G. Eysenbach[4]. As the author suggests *e-health is an emerging field in the intersection of medical informatics, public health and business, referring to health services and information delivered or enhanced through the Internet and related technologies. In a broader sense, the term characterizes not only a technical development, but also a state-of-mind, a way of thinking, an attitude, and a commitment for networked, global thinking, to improve Health-care locally, regionally, and worldwide by using information and communication technology.*

information that resides in a variety of heterogeneous clinical information systems.
- *Health Monitoring and Surveillance* where Healthcare monitoring information systems have been implemented for the analysis and reporting of primary health data.

Specifically in the AI arena, many intelligent systems have been developed for the purpose of enhancing Health-care and provide better Health-care facilities. As expressed by many studies (such as [5],[6],[1],[9],[8], or [3]) intelligent system have been developed to assist doctors and patients.

The papers selected for this collection focus on applications of Agent technologies to Health-care developed in Europe under the sponsorship of the EU. The collaboration between both disciplines is probably gathering pace due to matching circumstances. Agents research is one of the most prolific AI areas, especially in the generation of practical solutions for real problems, and public and private Health-care business is in crisis worldwide, with a lot of problems looking for solutions. Therefore, very productive results are expected from applying Intelligent Agents' research and solutions to Health-care issues.

2. Agents Solutions for Health-care

Shaping Agent-based technology for the healthcare challenges has a momentum created by various converging demands and trends. The articles included in this book have been selected to illustrate research addressing solutions for three major Health-care areas. First, we have selected solutions for Health-care organizations overall. Then we have selected research centered on supporting the medical practitioners and other Health-care professionals. Finally we have considered solutions for the patients. If we recapitulate the contents of the articles, we can see exactly two articles per area.

2.1. Health-care Organizations

Considering as a whole, Health-care organizations are confronting rising costs, even as delivering poor or inconsistent quality and offering inadequate choices to their users. More than aim for cost-reductions the challenge is to obtain the right value for the money. But to offer the right service at the right cost to every user requires improvements in complex Health-care processes - from claim to deliver - extended across several public and private stakeholders - from insurers to general practitioners, specialized units, hospitals, or residential/homecare - and sharing patients' critical personal data.

Agent applications have demonstrated their suitability for intelligent logistic optimization and resource allocation, based on dynamic distributed information, and including negotiations between several actors. Health-care management have plenty of that kind of problems. Two papers of this volume illustrate applications of Agents to organ transplant management:

- *Applying PROVENANCE in Distributed Organ Transplant Management*. The paper on PROVENANCE present a new approach to both capture the distributed medical treatment of a patient in different Health-care institutions in an integrated, patient oriented way, and to register all meaningful events related to a patient's treatment for further analysis, not only for audit purposes but also for medical staff to detect problems in the medical processes (e.g. bottlenecks or lack of timely information). The main hypothesis is that trust in results produced by an agent-mediated distributed Health-care system can be increased if it can be known the provenance of each of the particular results (e.g. where the patient was treated, who has been involved in each medical treatment, who has taken decisions and which were the basis for such decisions). PROVENANCE awareness enables users to trace how and identifying the individual and aggregated services that produced a particular output has produced a particular result. This helps users to get an integrated view of the treatment process executed by distributed autonomous agents, and to be able to carry out audits of the system to assess that, for a given patient, the proper decisions were made and the proper procedures were followed.

- *ASPIC: Argumentation Service Platform with Integrated Components*. The main goals of ASPIC are (1) to develop a solid theoretical ground for the Argumentation Theory in Artificial Intelligence; (2) based on the theoretical work, develop practical-software components that embody standards for the argumentation-based technology (inference, decision-making, dialog and learning); and (3) in order to test these components develop one large scale demonstrator for organ selection and assignations. In ASPIC, the notion of autonomy will be used to denote the requirement that the software must have some ability to decide for itself which goals it should adopt and how these goals should be achieved. Classical logic based methods and quantitative algorithms are notoriously brittle in the face of uncertainty, ambiguity and incompleteness of knowledge in complex real-world situations, while decision-theoretic and other quantitative approaches lack the conceptual expressiveness and versatility of logical methods. The methodology of the project use argumentation in order to permit agents to treat the reasons that justify alternative goals and actions (arguments for and against) as first-class objects that can be explicitly analyzed, questioned and rebutted.

2.2. Professionals

In Health-care organizations, medical practitioners are facing a proliferation of patient's information coming from - or stored in - several institutions and including medical and non-medical data. There is a proportional increase of case information and reference data for diagnosis and treatment available on-line. Agent technologies can deal with this data flooding improving the quality of medical decision-making process whilst increasing patient compliance and minimizing iatrogenic disease and medical errors. It also improves the quality of assistance and offers new tools to support and monitor patients in daily activities. A couple of the selected papers illustrate this area:

- *SAPHIRE: A Multi-Agent System for Remote Health-care Monitoring through Computerized Clinical Guidelines.* SAPHIRE provides a Clinical Decision Support system for remote monitoring of patients at their homes, and at the hospital to decrease the load of medical practitioners and also Health-care costs. As the expert knowledge required building the clinical decision support system, Clinical Guidelines are exploited. The Agent Factory Agent processes the clinical guideline definitions represented in our extended model, and based on the semantic annotations of the external resources, discovers the instances of the specified resources that are relevant for each patient. This process can be summarized as follows (1) In SAPHIRE architecture, the medical Web services exposing functionalities of Health-care information systems, and also the sensor Web services exposing the sensor data retrieved from wireless medical sensor devices are published to a UDDI registry by annotating them with their functionality semantics. Whenever the Agent Factory encounters a reference to a medical procedure, it locates the medical procedures from UDDI service registries by their functionality that has been specified in the extended GLIF model. (2) Whenever the Agent Factory encounters a reference to a clinical data of patient to be retrieved from an EHR document, it sends a message to the EHR agent presenting the Document type, and Entry type semantics presented in the extended GLIF model. As a response a set of document identifiers are received pointing to relevant EHR documents.

- *Health Agents: Agent-based Distributed Decision Support System for Brain Tumor Diagnosis and Prognosis.* Using its Multi-Agent architecture, Health Agents applies cutting-edge agent technology to the Biomedical field and develop the Health Agents network, a globally distributed information and knowledge repository for brain tumor diagnosis and prognosis. The Health Agents project also develop the first distributed repository for brain tumor diagnosis, leading eventually to the formation of a special interest data grid.

2.3. Patients

Finally, there are also Intelligent Agents applications centered on the patients. Again, two of the selected papers cover this area:

- *K4CARE: Knowledge-Based Homecare e-services for an Ageing Europe.* The K4CARE approach offers a Knowledge-Based system to support assertive services for individuals living in their houses, namely Home Care services. Services in K4CARE use in a very extensively way clinical data stores in EHCR that provide the appropriate information to support the decision-making. The K4CARE platform will provide services to its users like patients, family doctors, physicians in charge, nurses, head nurses, social workers, etc. Each user will achieve its goals with the help of a set of services specific to his or her user type. A set of services specific to a user type will be incorporated in an agent. The agents may be distributed in the computer network. The services will invoke other services and thus the K4CARE platform will have a distributed service-oriented architecture. Some of the services will correspond to medical processes and their execution procedures will be based on medical guidelines (i.e. evidence-based medicine), while other services will correspond to administrative or technical procedures related to the operation of the platform or the home care center.

- *Supported Human Autonomy for Recovery and Enhancement of cognitive and motor disabilities using Agent technologies.* The main objective of SHARE-it is to develop a scalable, adaptive system of add-ons to sensor and assistive technology so that they can be modularly integrated into an intelligent home environment to enhance individual's autonomy. The system will be designed to inform and assist the user and his/her caregivers through monitoring and mobility help. Thus, it plans to contribute to the development of the next generation of assistive devices for older persons or people with disabilities so that they can be self-dependent as long as possible. It focus on add-ons to be compatible with existing technologies and to achieve an easier integration into existing systems. We also aim at adaptive systems as transparent, and consequently, easy to use to the person as possible. Scalability is meant to include or remove devices from the system in a simple, intuitive way. SHARE-it will provide an Agent-based Intelligent Decision Support System to aid the elders.

Patients support, especially elder or disable patients, will probably be the most important challenge for the near future in all countries. In "an aging world" [7] Agent-base solutions and assistive technologies will have a key role.

3. Assistive Technologies for Elderly and Physical and Cognitive Impaired People

There is a global trend of increasing longevity in our societies as the human life span is expanded. More people live longer and, due to the progresses of medicine, many more survive acute diseases but affected by chronic conditions and some disabilities.

The main effort of scientific research in this area is to guarantee the autonomy of this population in order to obtain two important results: firstly improve patients and cargivers' life quality, and secondly allow elderly people to live at home as long as possible. New technology can help people affected by physical and cognitive impairments, functional loss from multiple disabilities and impaired self-dependency of different degrees.

Persons with cognitive disabilities can benefit from a number of aids. These aids can assist the person by enhancing his or her performance of functional tasks that have become more difficult because of impaired memory or retrieval of information, impaired comprehension, or difficulties understanding cause and effect. Assistive technologies can also aid in modifying such behavioral problems as impulsive decision making and poor management of daily routines (e.g., missed appointments) that are often directly attributable to cognitive changes such as decreased memory, organization capabilities, or plannification.

Persons with physical disabilities related with mobility are prevalent in the older population. Interventions to cope with mobility disability are of three basic types: improve the individual's ability to perform the activity by mending the diseases or impairments causing the disability, eliminate the need to perform the activity or parts of the activity through use of personal assistance, or alter the way the activity is performed, for example through use of assistive technology such as cane, walker or wheelchair. Use of assistive technology is an increasingly common way of coping with disabilities.

Some research has focused on robotics-based wheelchairs yielding sensors to assist their users both in cognitive and physical disabilities. The use of agent technology in this field is opening new ways of interaction with the patients. The ultimate goal of the interaction between robotics, agent systems and the users is to enhance autonomy and upgrade the quality and complexity of services offered.

By enabling a person to perform desired tasks, assistive technologies have also the potential to provide a sense of competence and re-connection to the community. By accommodating a person's weaknesses and supporting his or her strengths, assistive technologies can reduce psychosocial stressors, thus leading to renewed confidence and self-esteem.

4. Conclusions: A Glance to the Future

According with Altman, the future for medicine will be better and better [2]. A key factor of this continuous improvement will be the smart use of computation and communication tools to support Health-care organizations, the medical practice, caregiver professionals, and the relationship of all those actors with their patients.

A key componet of this "smart use of computation" will be the use of Agent technology. As we have explained, Agents can improve Health-care organizations and can support doctors and caregivers. However, the impact of the use of Agent technology with patients will not only be an improvement but a radical change in how Health-care and assistance will be provided to this population segment.

To achieve this radical change, it will be especially important to address the needs of elderly, and physical and cognitive impaired, patients. As explained, the autonomy of this kind of population is important to improve their quality of life. But allow elderly people to live at home as long as possible is also needed to deal with the demographic explosion of this segment of the population and with the overhead that it will suppose to the Health-care and social assistance systems.

The use of Agents in supporting of independent living, wellness and disease management, will make Healthcare and assistance services available everywhere, anytime and to everybody. The use of authonomous Agents in the delivery of healthcare to citizens will also raise numerous challenges. For example, new solutions will be needed for dealing with personal, sensitive health-related aspects of a person's life.

In conclusion, the role of Agent technology in Healthcare and assistence delivery will be vast and the realization process of the potential has just begun.

References

[1] Alexopoulos, E., Dounias, G. D., and Vemmos, K. (1999). *Medical Diagnosis of Stroke Using Inductive Machine Learning.* Machine Learning and Applications: Machine Learning in Medical Applications. Chania, Greece, pp. 20-23.

[2] Altman, R. B. (1999). *AI in Medicine: The Spectrum of Challenges from Managed Care to molecular Medicine.* AI Magazine, Vol. 20, No. 3, pp. 67 - 77.

[3] Bourlas, P., Giakoumakis, E., and Papakonstantinou, G. (1999). *A Knowledge Acquisition and management System for ECG Diagnosis.* Machine Learning and Applications: Machine Learning in Medical Applications. Chania, Greece, pp. 27-29.

[4] Eysenbach G . *What is e-health?.* J Med Internet Res 2001;3(suppl 2):e20. URL: http://www.jmir.org/2001/2/e20/

[5] Mahabala, H. N., Chandrasekhara, M. K., Baskar, S., Ramesh, S., and Somasundaram, M. S. (1992). *ICHT: An Intelligent Referral System for Primary Child Health Care.* Proceedings SEARCC'92: XI Conference of the South East Asia Regional Computer Confederation. Kuala Lumpur.

[6] Manickam, S., and Abidi, S. S. R. (1999). *Experienced Based Medical Diagnostics System Over The World Wide Web (WWW).* Proceedings of The First National Conference on Artificial Intelligence Application In Industry, Kuala Lumpur, pp. 47 - 56.

[7] Pollack, M.E. (2005). *Intelligent Technologies for an Aging Population.* AI Magazine Summer 2005.

[8] Ruseckaite, R. (1999). *Computer Interactive System for Ascertainment of Visual Perception Disorders.* Machine Learning and Applications: Machine Learning in Medical Applications. Chania, Greece, pp. 27-29.

[9] Zelic, I., Lavrac, N., Najdenov, P., Rener-Primec, Z. (1999). *Impact of machine Learning of the Diagnosis and Prognosis of First Cerebral Paroxysm.* Machine Learning and Applications: Machine Learning in Medical Applications. Chania, Greece, pp. 24-26.

Alfredo Villar
Universitat Politècnica de Catalunya
Barcelona
Spain
e-mail: alfredo.villar@gmail.com

Alessia Federici
Fondazione Santa Lucia
Via Ardetina 306
Roma, Italia
e-mail: a.federici@hsantalucia.it

Roberta Annicchiarico
Fondazione Santa Lucia
Via Ardetina 306
Roma, Italia
e-mail: r.annicchiarico@hsantalucia.it

Whitestein Series in Software Agent Technologies and Autonomic Computing

Edited by

Marius Walliser, Stefan Brantschen, Monique Calisti and Stefan Schinkinger

This series reports new developments in agent-based software technologies and agent-oriented software engineering methodologies, with particular emphasis on applications in the area of autonomic computing and communications.
The spectrum of the series includes research monographs, high quality notes resulting from research and industrial projects, outstanding Ph.D. theses, and the proceedings of carefully selected conferences. The series is targeted at promoting advanced research and facilitating know-how transfer to industrial use.

BIRKHÄUSER

■ **Calisti, M.**, Whitestein Technologies AG, Zürich, Switzerland / **van der Meer, S.**, Waterford Institute of Technology, Ireland / **Strassner, J.**, Motorola, Inc., Schaumburg, IL, USA (eds.)

Advanced Autonomic Networking and Communication

This book presents a comprehensive reference of state-of-the-art efforts and early results in the area of autonomic networking and communication.
The essence of autonomic networking, and thus autonomic communications, is to enable the self-governing of services and resources within the constraints of business rules. In order to support self-governance, appropriate self-* functionality will be deployed in the network on an application-specific basis. The continuing increase in complexity of upcoming networking convergence scenarios mandates a new approach to network management.
This volume explores different ways that autonomic principles can be applied to existing and future networks. In particular, the book has 3 main parts, each of them represented by three papers discussing them from industrial and academic perspectives.
The first part focuses on architectures and modeling strategies. Part two is dedicated to middleware and service infrastructure as facilitators of autonomic communications, and the last part addresses autonomic networks, specifically how current networks can be equipped with autonomic functionality and thus migrate to autonomic networks.

2007. 200 pages. Softcover.
ISBN 978-3-7643-8568-2

■ **Annicchiarico, R.**, Fondazione Santa Lucia IRCCS, Rome, Italy / **Cortés, U.**, Universidad Malaga, Spain / **Urdiales, C.**, Universidad Polytècnica de Catalunya, Barcelona, Spain (eds.)

Agent Technology and e-Health

2007. 156 pages. Softcover.
ISBN 978-3-7643-8546-0

■ **Pĕchouček, M.**, Czech Technical University, Prague, Czech Republic / **Thompson, S.G.**, BT. Labs, Suffolk, U.K. / **Voos, H.**, University of Applied Sciences, Ravensburg-Weingarten, Germany (eds.)

Defense Industry Applications of Autonomous Agents and Multi-Agent Systems

Defense and security related applications are increasingly being tackled by researchers and practioners using technologies developed in the field of Intelligent Agent research. This book is a collection of recent refereed papers drawn from workshops and other colloquia held in various venues around the world in the last two years.
The contributions in this book describe work in the development of command and control systems, military communications systems, information systems, surveillance systems, autonomous vehicles, simulators and Human Computer Interactions. The broad nature of the application domain is matched by the diversity of techniques used in the papers that are included in the collection which provides, for the first time, an overview of the most significant work being performed by the leading workers in this area. It provides a single reference point for the state of the art in the field at the moment and will be of interest to Computer Science professionals working in the defense sector, and academics and students investigating the technology of Intelligent Agents that are curious to see how the technology is applied in practice.

2007. 180 pages. Softcover.
ISBN 978-3-7643-8570-5

■ **Moreno, A.** University of Tarragona, Spain / **Pavón, J.**, University of Madrid, Spain (eds.)

**Issues in Multi-Agent Systems
The AgentCities.ES Experience**

The agent paradigm has been a subject of research for the last years, and the purpose of this book is to present current status of this technology by looking at its application in different domains, such as electronic markets, e-tourism, ambience intelligence, and complex system analysis.

2007. 240 pages. Softcover.
ISBN 978-3-7643-8542-2

■ **Pautasso, C.**, IBM Zürich, Switzerland / **Bussler, C.**, Cisco Systems Inc., San Jose, USA (eds.)

Emerging Web Services Technology

2007. 182 pages. Softcover.
ISBN 978-3-7643-8447-0